Maths Progress
Support Book

Series editors: Dr Naomi Norman and Katherine Pate
Authors: Sharon Bolger, Catherine Murphy and Amy O'Brien

1

Pearson

Maths Progress Second Edition

Confidence at the heart

Maths Progress Second Edition is built around a unique pedagogy that has been created by leading mathematics, educational researchers and Key Stage 3 teachers in the UK. The result is an innovative structure, based around 10 key principles designed to nurture confidence and raise achievement.

Pedagogy – our 10 key principles

- Fluency
- Problem-solving
- Reflection
- Mathematical Reasoning
- Progression
- Linking
- Multiplicative Reasoning
- Modelling
- Concrete - Pictorial - Abstract (CPA)
- Relevance

This edition of Maths Progress has been updated based on feedback from thousands of teachers and students.

The Core Curriculum

Textbooks with tried-and-tested differentiation

Core Textbooks *For your whole cohort*

Based on a single, well-paced curriculum with built-in differentiation, fluency, problem-solving and reasoning so you can use them with your whole class. They follow the unique unit structure that's been shown to boost confidence and support every student's progress.

Support Books
Strengthening skills and knowledge

Provide extra scaffolding and support on key concepts for each lesson in the Core Textbook, giving students the mathematical foundations they need to progress with confidence.

Depth Books
Extending skills and knowledge

Deepen students' understanding of key concepts, and build problem-solving skills for each lesson in the Core Textbook so students can explore key concepts to their fullest.

Welcome to Maths Progress Second Edition Support Books!

Master
Learn fundamental knowledge and skills over a series of lessons.

Key point Explain key concepts and definitions where students need them.

Hints Guide students to help build problem-solving strategies throughout the course.

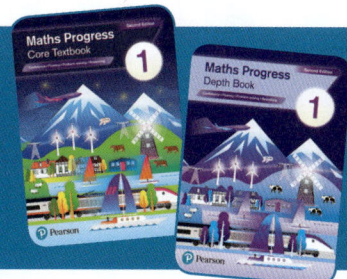

Worked example Provides guidance around examples of key concepts with images, bar models, and other pictorial representations where needed.

Reflect Metacognitive questions that ask students to examine their thinking and understanding.

Guided questions
Provide extra scaffolding or partially completed answers to help students work through questions step by step.

The Support Book is designed to give students additional scaffolding and support on key concepts contained in each Core Textbook lesson. It gives students the mathematical foundations they need to progress with confidence.
Depth books are available for students who would benefit from additional problem-solving content and further stretch.

Progress with confidence!

This innovative Key Stage 3 Mathematics course builds on the first edition KS3 Maths Progress (2014) course, drawing on input from thousands of teachers and students, and a 2-year study into the effectiveness of the course. All of this has come together with the latest cutting-edge approaches to shape Maths Progress Second Edition.

Take a look at the other parts of the series

*Active*Learn Service

The *Active*Learn service enhances the course by bringing together your planning, teaching and assessment tools, as well as giving students access to additional resources to support their learning. Use the interactive Scheme of Work, linked to all the teacher and student resources, to create a personalised learning experience both in and outside the classroom.

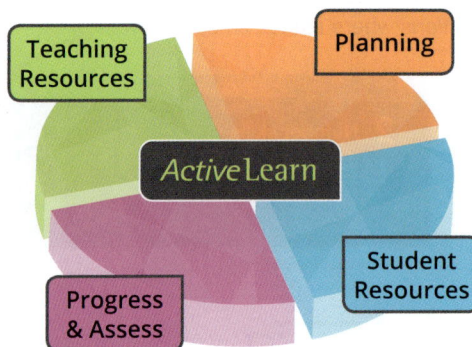

Teaching Resources

Planning

*Active*Learn

Student Resources

Progress & Assess

What's in ActiveLearn for Maths Progress?

- ☑ **Front-of-class student books** with links to PowerPoints, videos, animations and homework activities

- ☑ **96 new KS3 assessments and online markbooks,** including end-of-unit, end-of-term and end-of-year tests

- ☑ **Over 500 editable and printable homework worksheets** linked to each lesson and differentiated for Support, Core and Depth

- ☑ **Online, auto-marked homework activities**

- ☑ **Interactive Scheme of Work** makes re-ordering the course easy by bringing everything together into one curriculum for all students with links to Core, Support and Depth resources, and teacher guidance

- ☑ **Student access to videos, homework and online textbooks**

ActiveLearn Progress & Assess

The Progress & Assess service is part of the full ActiveLearn service, or can be bought as a separate subscription. It includes assessments that have been designed to ensure all students have the opportunity to show what they have learned through:

- a 2-tier assessment model
- approximately 60% common questions from Core in each tier
- separate calculator and non-calculator sections
- online markbooks for tracking and reporting
- mapped to indicative 9–1 grades

New *Assessment Builder*

Create your own classroom assessments from the bank of Maths Progress assessment questions by selecting questions on the skills and topics you have covered. Map the results of your custom assessments to indicative 9–1 grades using the custom online markbooks. *Assessment Builder* is available to purchase as an add-on to the *Active*Learn Service or Progress & Assess subscriptions.

Purposeful Practice Books

Over 3,750 questions using minimal variations that:

- ☑ build in small steps to consolidate knowledge and boost confidence
- ☑ focus on strengthening skills and strategies, such as problem-solving
- ☑ help every student put their learning into practice in different ways
- ☑ give students a strong preparation for progressing to GCSE study

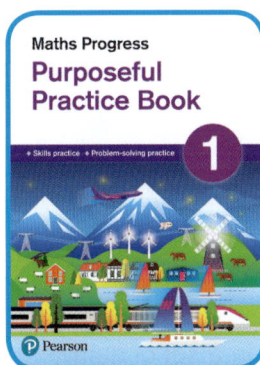

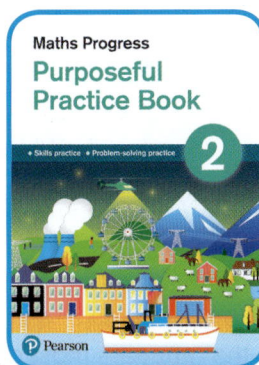

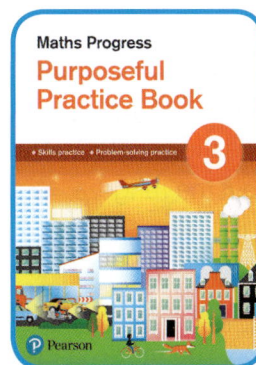

1   Analysing and displaying data

1.1   Mode, median and range

- Find the mode, median and range for a set of data

Range

> **Key point**   The **range** shows how spread out a set of data is.
>
> range = largest value – smallest value

Guided

1   This data is written in order, from smallest to largest.

     5, 8, 8, 12, 14

   a   Write the largest value.   **b**   Write the smallest value.

   c   Work out the range: largest value – smallest value = range

                   □   –   □   =   □

Guided

2   Here is a set of data.

     10, 5, 2, 7, 2

   a   Order the values from smallest to largest: 2, 2, □, □, □

   b   Copy and complete to work out the range. Range = □ – □ = □

3   For each set of data, order the values from smallest to largest, then work out the range.

   a   12, 20, 13, 10, 5   **b**   32, 23, 12, 10   **c**   8, 15, 30, 21

4   Some Year 7 students counted the number of text messages they got in one day.

     6, 4, 7, 12, 3, 10, 5

   a   Which is the smallest value?   **b**   Which is the largest value?

   c   Work out the range.

Mode

> **Key point**   The **mode** is the item that appears most often in a set of data.

1   Leo and his friends chose their favourite colour.

     blue, green, green, red, yellow, orange

   Which colour is the most popular? This is the mode.

2   Abida and her friends chose their favourite colour.

     blue, green, red, blue, yellow, blue, orange, blue

   Which colour is the mode?

3 Here are Julian's marks in six maths tests.

8, 12, 12, 13, 15, 16

What mark is the mode?

4 Write the mode of each set of data.

a 5, 4, 0, 5, 4, 0, 2, 4

b 15, 20, 14, 14, 12, 10, 14

5 Write the mode for each set of values.

a win, draw, win, lose, lose, lose, win, draw, win, lose, win, win, draw

b 3, 4, 7, 5, 0, 6, 2, 4, 5, 4, 0

Median

> **Key point** The **median** is the middle value when the data is written in order.

1 **a** The diagram shows some crayons arranged in order of size.
Write the length of the middle crayon. This is the median.

b Here are the lengths of another set of crayons:

2 cm, 2 cm, 3 cm, 6 cm, 7 cm

Find the median.

3 cm   4 cm   6 cm   7 cm   8 cm

Guided

2 This set of data is ordered from smallest to largest.

2 cm, 5 cm, 8 cm, 10 cm, 12 cm, 13 cm, 15 cm

a Copy the data. Cross off values from each end, in pairs, to find the middle one. One pair has already been crossed off.

~~2 cm~~, 5 cm, 8 cm, 10 cm, 12 cm, 13 cm, ~~15 cm~~

b Write the middle value. This is the median.

3 Write each set of data in order from smallest to largest. Find the median of each set.

a 4, 6, 5, 3, 7

b 9, 12, 18, 7, 8, 14, 16

c 12, 20, 19, 14, 11

d 20, 10, 40, 60, 30, 50, 30

4 This set of data has two middle values.

~~2~~, ~~3~~, 3, 5, ~~7~~ ~~9~~

Write the value in the middle of the two values. This is the median.

5 Find the median of each set of data.

a 3, 5, 7, 10

b 2, 4, 8, 10, 12, 13

> **Reflect** Why is it helpful to order numbers from smallest to largest before finding the median, mode and range?

1.2 Displaying data

* Find information from tables and diagrams
* Display data using tally charts, tables and bar charts

Pictograms

1 The pictogram shows the number of pieces of fruit that Mark ate in one week.

Fruit eaten in a week

a How many apples did he eat?

b Copy and complete the sentence.
The fruit Mark ate most was _____

c How many bananas did he eat?

Key: ⬤ represents 1 piece of fruit

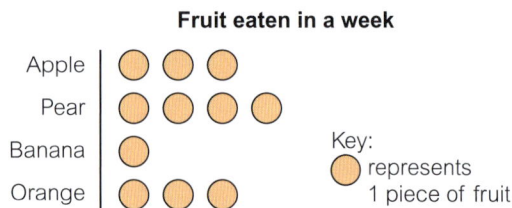

2 The pictogram shows some students' favourite sports.

Favourite sports

a How many students like football?

b How many students like tennis?

c How many students like running?

Key: ▯ represents 2 students

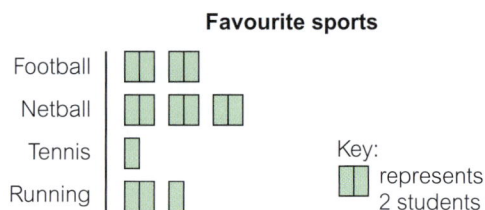

3 The pictogram shows the colour of cars that passed by a school in one day.

Colour of cars

a How many green cars passed by the school?

b How many red cars passed by the school?

c **Problem-solving** How many cars does ◖ represent?

d Which colour of car passed by the school most? This is the mode.

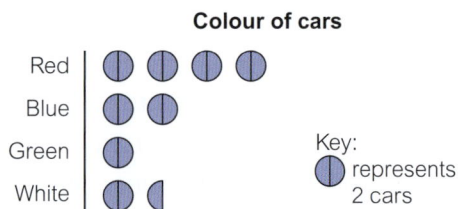

Key: ⬤ represents 2 cars

Bar charts

1 What is the interval between the numbers on each scale?

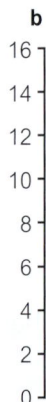

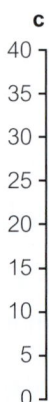

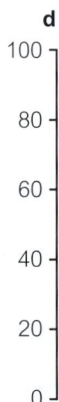

3

2 Problem-solving The bar chart shows the favourite activities of Year 7 students at a leisure centre.

Y7 favourite activity

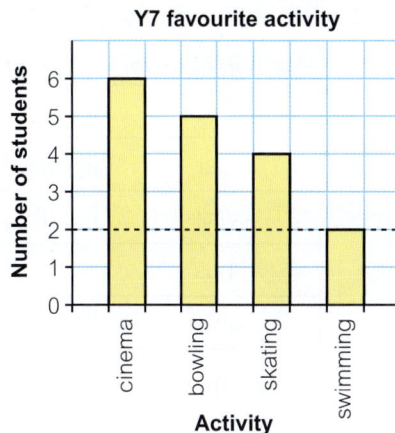

a Put your finger on top of the bar for swimming. Follow the dotted line to the vertical axis. Read off the value. This tells you how many students chose swimming.

Copy and complete this sentence.

☐ students chose swimming.

b Which is the most popular activity?

c i How many students chose bowling?

ii How many students chose cinema?

iii How many more students chose cinema than bowling?

3 Year 8 students chose these activities as their favourite.

Activity	Number of students
cinema	6
bowling	4
skating	2
swimming	3

Y8 favourite activity

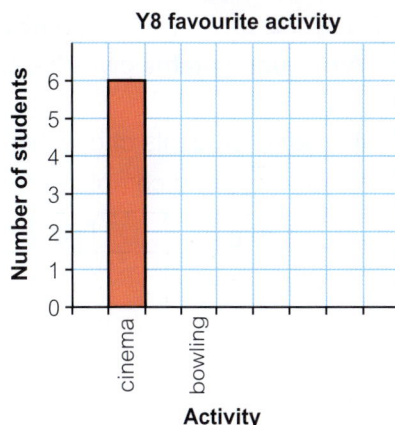

a Copy and complete the bar chart to show all the data in the table. Make sure all bars are the same width and there is a gap between them.

b Give your bar chart a title.

4 Problem-solving The bar chart shows the sales of laptop cases.

Laptop case sales

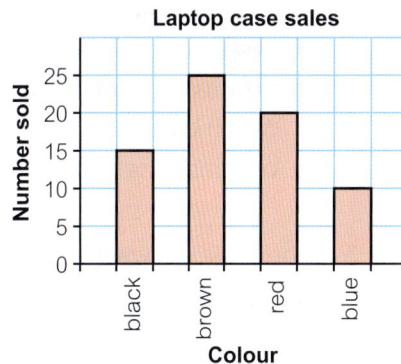

a How many blue cases were sold?

b How many red cases were sold?

c How many more red cases were sold than blue cases?

d How many cases were sold altogether?

e Which colour case has the tallest bar? This is the mode.

Tally charts and frequency tables

> **Key point**
> You can record data in a **tally chart**. Use a **tally** mark | for each value.
> Group tally marks in 5s like this: ⦀⦀

1 Count the tally marks.

a |||| b ⦀⦀ ⦀⦀   c ⦀⦀ ⦀⦀ ||

2 Draw tally marks to represent these numbers.

a 3   b 7   c 14

3 Problem-solving This tally chart shows how some Year 7 students travel to school.

Method of travel	Tally
bicycle	||||
car	卌 卌 ||||
walk	卌 卌 卌 |||
bus	
other	|||

a How many students cycle to school?   b How many walk to school?

c 21 students travel by bus. Draw the tally marks for this.

d A student is picked from Year 7. What is the most likely way they travel to school?

Key point   The **frequency** is the number of times something happens.
A **frequency table** gives the frequency for each item.

---

4 Some students chose their favourite big cat.

a Copy and complete the frequency table.

Big cat	Tally	Frequency
lion		12
tiger	卌 ||	
cheetah	|||	
leopard	卌		
jaguar	卌	

b How many students chose jaguar?

c Which big cat was chosen by 7 students?

d Which big cat was most popular?

5 The table shows the numbers of boys and girls who play tennis.

Players	Frequency
Boys	10
Girls	15
Total	25

a How many boys are there?

b How many students are there altogether?

c How many more girls than boys are there?

Reflect   Look back at **Pictograms Q1** and **Bar charts Q3**.
How do you find the mode from a pictogram?
How do you find it from a bar chart?

1.3 Grouping data

- Interpret simple charts for grouped data
- Find the modal class for grouped data

Grouped tally charts and frequency tables

> **Key point** Data is sometimes put into **groups** or **classes**, such as, 1–4, 5–8, 9–12, …
> The group 1–4 consists of 1, 2, 3 and 4.
> A **grouped frequency table** gives the frequency for each group.

Worked example

Graham recorded the number of emails the students in his class sent each week.

4, 8, 5, 7, 7, 8, 2, 2, 3, 3, 10, 5, 7, 6, 7, 7, 15, 12, 9 — The first number is 4. Make a tally mark for the group 1–4. Cross the number 4 off the list.

a Complete the grouped frequency table for this data.

Number of emails	Tally	Frequency
1–4	卌	5
5–8	卌 卌	10
9–12	|||	3
13–16			1

Count the tally marks and write the answer in the frequency column.

b How many people sent 9–12 emails?

3

c Which is the modal group? — The modal group is the one with the highest frequency.

5–8 emails

1 Copy this table.
Complete your table for this set of data.
5, 11, 3, 8, 4, 12, 10, 2, 5, 12, 7, 2, 6, 1

Group	Tally	Frequency
1–3		
4–6		
7–9		
10–12		

2 A teacher records the number of books in students' school bags.

3, 5, 4, 7, 4, 7, 5, 2, 5, 5, 7, 8, 2, 2, 4, 3, 5, 5, 10

The teacher draws this grouped frequency table.

Number of books	Tally	Frequency
1–3		
4–6		
7–9		
10–12		

a Copy the table. Tally the number of books in the table. Fill in the frequency column.

b Write the group with a tally of

   i 5 books   ii 9 books

c Which is the modal group?

Bar charts for grouped data

1 The grouped bar chart shows the number of marks that students got in a maths test.

a What marks are included in the 5–9 group?

b How many students achieved 10–14 marks?

c Which group has the most students?

Maths test marks

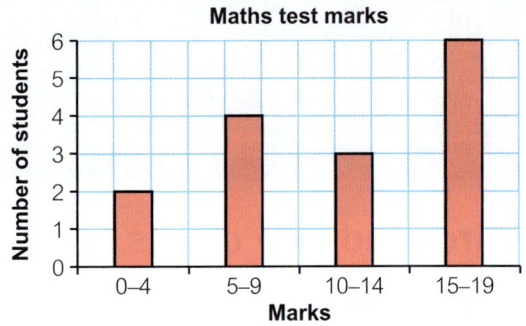

2 This bar chart shows the number of phone calls made by a Year 8 class last month.

a How many students made between 1 and 5 phone calls?

b How many students made more than 10 phone calls?

Number of phone calls made last month

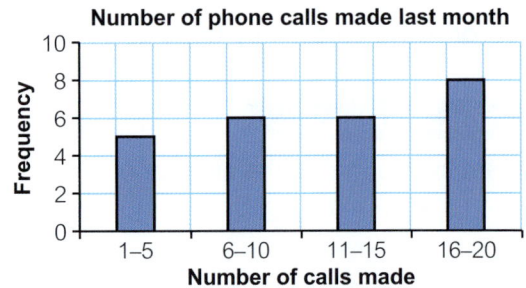

3 Elena investigated the numbers of books students owned. She recorded her results in a grouped frequency table.

a Which group has the highest frequency?

b Copy and complete the grouped bar chart for the data.

Number of books	Frequency
0–4	8
5–9	12
10–14	6
15–19	6
20–24	2
25–29	2

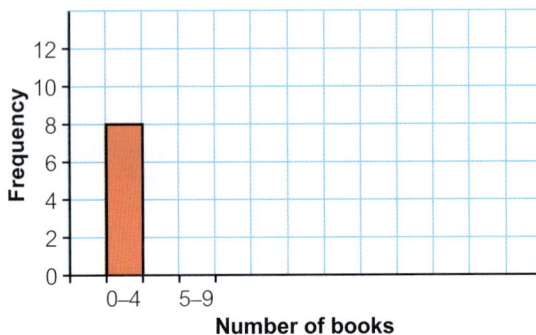

4 The bar chart shows the height of plants a gardener has in the garden, to the nearest centimetre.

a How many plants are in the 10–19 group?

b How many plants are in the 0–9 group?

c How many plants are there altogether?

Height of plants in garden

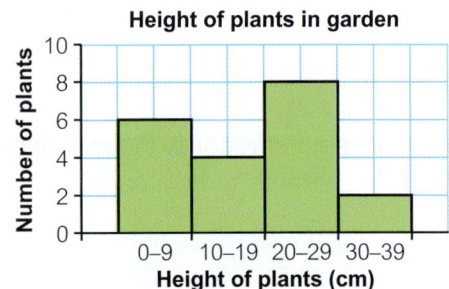

Reflect Look at **Q3** with a partner.

Which group would the value 19 be in?

1.4 Averages and comparing data

- Calculate the mean of a set of data
- Compare sets of data using their ranges and averages

Mean

Worked example

Four siblings have this amount of money in their pockets: £2, £2, £3, £5
How much do they have altogether?
£2 + £2 + £3 + £5 = £12
The money is shared out equally between them.
How much do they each get?
This is the mean.
£12 ÷ 4 = £3

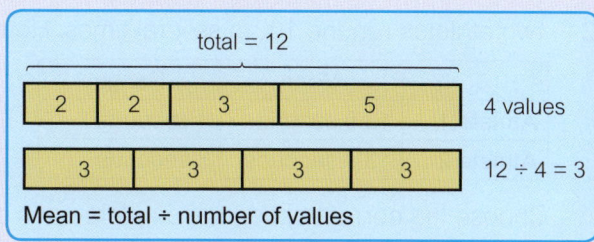

total = 12

| 2 | 2 | 3 | 5 | 4 values |

| 3 | 3 | 3 | 3 | 12 ÷ 4 = 3 |

Mean = total ÷ number of values

Guided

1 Copy and complete the workings below to find the mean for each set of values.

a 4 2

$(4 + 2) ÷ 2 = \Box ÷ 2$

$\qquad\qquad = \Box$

b 7 5 9

$(\Box + \Box + \Box) ÷ 3 = \Box ÷ 3$

$\qquad\qquad\qquad = \Box$

c 4 6 5 1

$(\Box + \Box + \Box + \Box) ÷ 4 = \Box ÷ 4$

$\qquad\qquad\qquad\qquad = \Box$

d 1 2 2 2 3

$(\Box + \Box + \Box + \Box + \Box) ÷ 5 = \Box ÷ 5$

$\qquad\qquad\qquad\qquad\qquad = \Box$

2 Here is a set of values: 9, 3, 5, 0, 2
   a Use your calculator to add up the values.
   b How many values are there?
   c Work out the mean.

> **Q2c hint** Divide the total by the number of values. $\Box ÷ \Box = \Box$

3 Four children brought these numbers of sparklers to a party.
   8   15   9   12
   a Work out the total number of sparklers.
   b They shared the sparklers equally. How many sparklers did each child get?
   c What is the mean number of sparklers?

4 Sarah has £1 and Jess has £4.
   a Work out how much money they have in total.
   b They share the money equally. How much does each person get?
   c What is the mean amount of money?

Comparing sets of data

1 **Problem-solving** In a science lesson some students measured their heights.

152 cm, 142 cm, 147 cm, 138 cm, 152 cm, 145 cm

Work out

a the mode   b the median   c the mean   d the range

2 Two athletes run the 100 m several times. Here are the means and ranges of their times.

	Mean	Range
Athlete 1	12.5 seconds	4 seconds
Athlete 2	13.1 seconds	3 seconds

Choose the correct option to complete each of these sentences.

a The mean for athlete 1 is larger than/smaller than/the same as the mean for athlete 2.

b The range for athlete 1 is larger than/smaller than/the same as the range for athlete 2.

c The times for athlete 1 are less spread/more spread than the times for athlete 2.

3 Here are the numbers of goals scored in 8 matches by two football clubs.

Club A   3, 4, 3, 2, 3, 3, 3, 3

Club B   2, 2, 2, 1, 3, 4, 4, 6

a Work out the mean number of goals for each club.

b Work out the range of the number of goals for each club.

c Copy and complete this table for the two clubs.

	Mean	Range
Club A		
Club B		

d Choose the correct option to complete each of these sentences.

   i The mean for club A is larger than/smaller than/the same as the mean of club B.

   ii The range for club A is larger than/smaller than/the same as the range for club B, so the number of goals for club A is less spread/more spread than the number of goals for club B.

1.5 Line graphs and more bar charts

- Understand and draw line graphs
- Understand dual and compound bar charts

Line graphs

Key point Line graphs show how quantities change.

Worked example

The line graph shows the number of ice cream sales made in a café in the first half of the year.

Ice cream sales

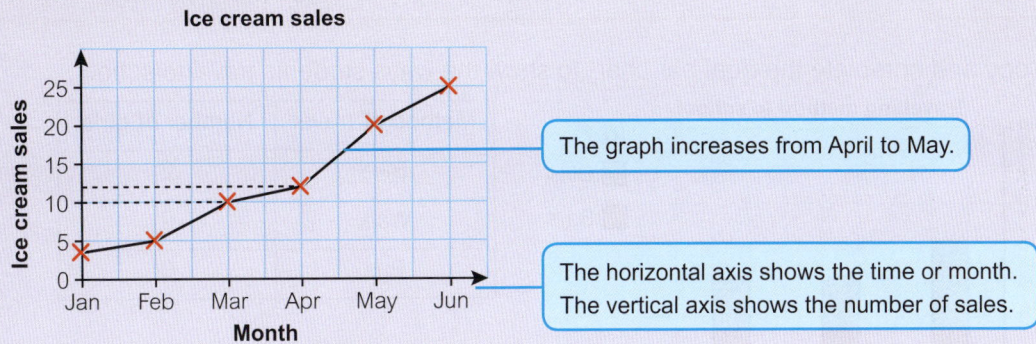

The graph increases from April to May.

The horizontal axis shows the time or month. The vertical axis shows the number of sales.

a How many ice cream sales were made in March?

10

b How many ice cream sales were made in April?

12

c Did ice cream sales increase or decrease between April and May?

Increase

1 **Problem-solving** This line graph shows the number of cars in a car park one morning.

Cars in a car park

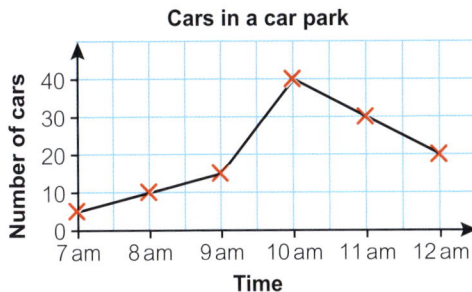

Q1 hint If the graph slopes upwards, the number is increasing. If it slopes downwards, the number is decreasing.

a What was the maximum number of cars in the car park?
b At what time were there 10 cars in the car park?
c Did the number of cars increase or decrease between 10 am and 11 am?
d Did the number of cars increase or decrease between 8 am and 9 am?

2 The table shows the number of emails Marcus received in one week.

Day	Number of emails
Mon	3
Tue	2
Wed	2
Thu	4
Fri	5

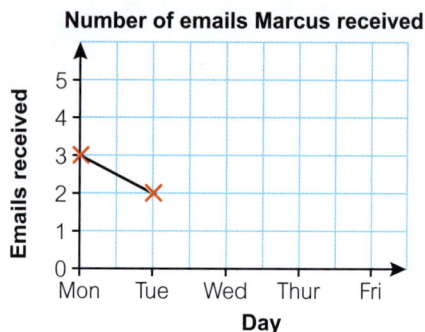

Complete the line graph of the number of emails Marcus received. It has been started for you.

Number of emails Marcus received

Dual bar charts

> **Key point** A dual bar chart shows two sets of data on the same graph.

1 a Copy and complete the dual bar chart to show the ways students travel to school.

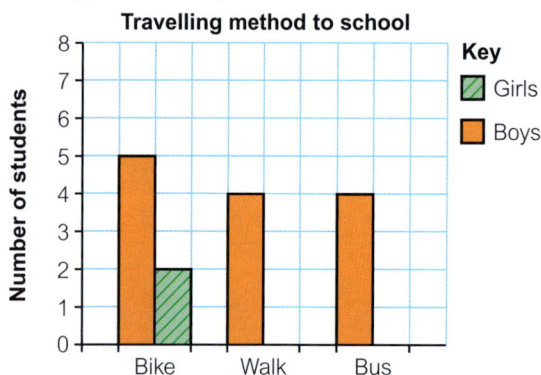

Travelling method to school

Key
- Girls
- Boys

Method of travel	Number of girls
Bike	2
Walk	8
Bus	0

b Reasoning Why did you not draw a bar for the number of girls who travel by bus?

2 The dual bar chart shows the colours of students' mobile phone covers.

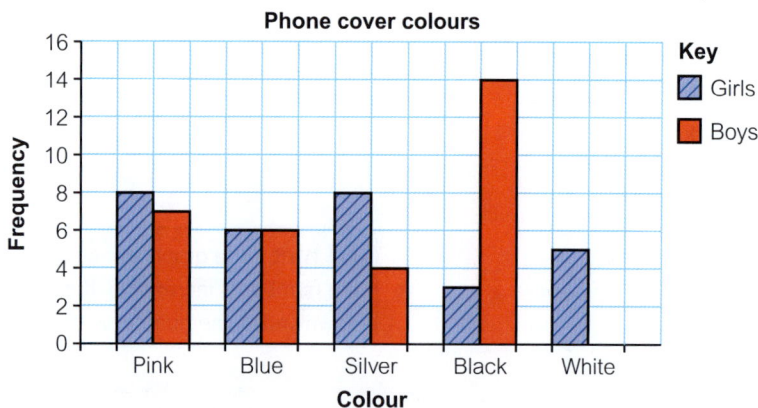

Phone cover colours

Key
- Girls
- Boys

a How many girls have a black mobile phone cover?

b Which is the most popular colour for boys?

c Why does white only have one bar?

d How many more girls have a silver mobile phone cover than boys?

e Which colour of cover has the same number for girls and boys?

f What is the total number of girls?

11

Compound bar charts

Worked example

This compound bar chart shows the number of visitors to an art exhibition one weekend.

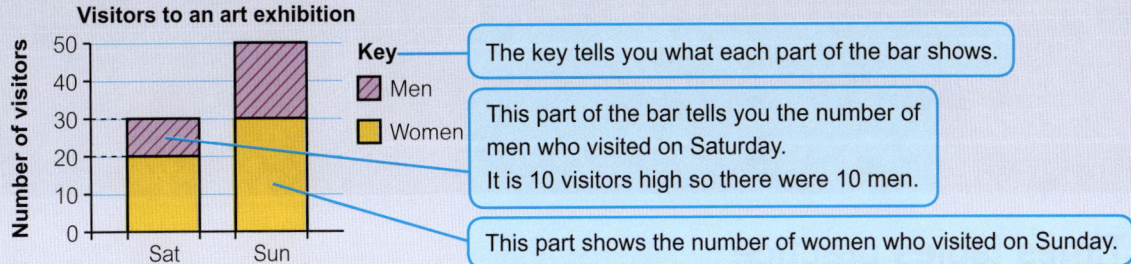

Visitors to an art exhibition

Key

The key tells you what each part of the bar shows.

▨ Men

☐ Women

This part of the bar tells you the number of men who visited on Saturday.
It is 10 visitors high so there were 10 men.

This part shows the number of women who visited on Sunday.

a How many women visited the exhibition on Sunday?

30

b How many men visited the exhibition over the weekend?

Saturday = 10   Sunday = 20

10 + 20 = 30

1 This compound bar chart shows the sales of computer games by a small company.

a How many shop sales were made in June?

b How many online sales were made in May?

c How many online sales were made in June and July?

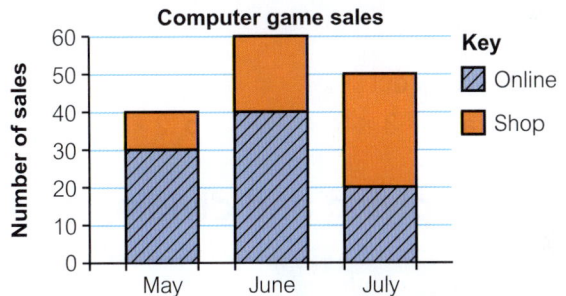

Computer game sales

Key

▨ Online

☐ Shop

2 The table shows the numbers of adults and children visiting a park during the summer.

	Adults	Children
June	20	30
July	30	40
August	20	40

a How many adults visited the park in June?

b Copy and complete the compound bar chart. Draw the bar for children in July first.

c In which month was there the greatest difference between adults and children?

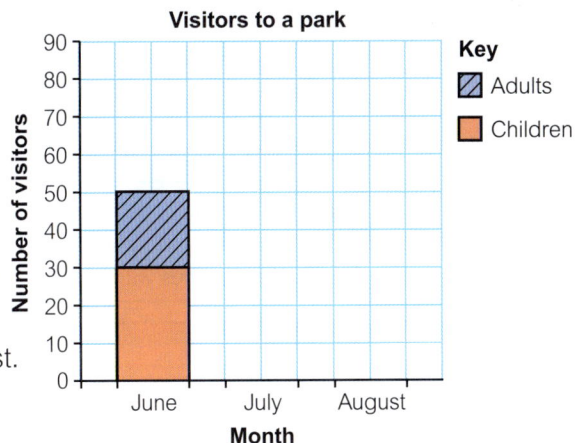

Visitors to a park

Key

▨ Adults

☐ Children

Reflect Look back at **Dual bar charts Q1** and **Compound bar charts Q1**.

Discuss with a partner the difference between a compound bar chart and a dual bar chart.

2   Number skills

2.1   Mental maths

- Use multiplication facts up to 10×10 and the laws of arithmetic to do mental multiplication and division
- Multiply and divide by 10, 100 and 1000
- Use the priority of operations

Times tables practice

1   Work out

    a 2×3 **b** 4×3 **c** 8×6 **d** 9×7

2   Find the missing numbers.

    a $4 \times \square = 12$ **b** $\square \times 9 = 36$ **c** $5 \times \square = 40$ **d** $\square \times 6 = 66$

    e $21 \div \square = 3$ **f** $15 \div \square = 3$ **g** $\square \div 3 = 7$ **h** $\square \div 8 = 5$

3   Work out

    a $2 \times 3 \times 5$ **b** $2 \times 3 \times 6$ **c** $4 \times 3 \times 6$

Multiplying and dividing by 10, 100 and 1000

Worked example

a   Work out 23×100

Thousands	Hundreds	Tens	Ones
		2	3
2	3	0	0

$23 \times 100 = 2300$

> $\times$ 100 makes the number 100 times larger. The digits move two places to the left ←. Fill any spaces with zeros.

b   Work out $450 \div 10$

Hundreds	Tens	Ones		tenths
4	5	0		
	4	5	.	0

$450 \div 10 = 45$

> $\div$ 10 makes the number 10 times smaller. The digits move one place to the right →.

1   Work out

    a 5×10 **b** 5×100 **c** 5×1000

    d 10×2 **e** 100×9 **f** 24×1000

2   Work out

    a $7000 \div 10$ **b** $7000 \div 100$ **c** $7000 \div 1000$

    d $2400 \div 100$ **e** $13\,000 \div 1000$ **f** $190 \div 10$

3 Work out

   a $20 = \Box \times 10$ **b** $30 = \Box \times 10$ **c** $400 = \Box \times 100$ **d** $6000 = \Box \times 1000$

Priority of operations

> **Key point**   Use the **priority of operations** (BIDMAS) to do calculations.
> Calculate division and multiplication before addition and subtraction.

> **Worked example**
>
> Calculate $3 + 2 \times 5$ $3 + \underbrace{2 \times 5}$ —— $\boxed{\text{Multiplication before addition}}$
>
> $= 3 + 10$
>
> $= 13$

Guided

1 Work out

   a $4 + \underbrace{2 \times 5}$ **b** $\underbrace{4 \times 6} + 10$ **c** $7 \times 4 + 1$ **d** $9 + 5 \times 4$

      $4 + 10$

> **Q1 hint** Multiplication before addition

Guided

2 Work out

   a $10 - \underbrace{2 \times 3}$ **b** $\underbrace{7 \times 5} - 11$ **c** $10 \times 3 - 12$ **d** $15 - 4 \times 2$

      $10 - 6$

> **Q2 hint** Multiplication before subtraction

Guided

3 Work out

   a $8 + \underbrace{20 \div 2}$ **b** $\underbrace{6 \div 3} + 11$ **c** $9 + 15 \div 3$ **d** $12 \div 4 + 8$

      $8 + 10$ 2

> **Q3 hint** Division before addition

Guided

4 Work out

   a $14 - \underbrace{8 \div 2}$ **b** $\underbrace{9 \div 3} - 2$ **c** $10 - 12 \div 2$ **d** $10 \div 5 - 1$

      $14 - 4$

> **Q4 hint** Division before subtraction

5 Work from left to right to calculate

   a $2 + 3 + 4$ **b** $4 + 2 + 3$ **c** $10 - 4 - 3$ **d** $10 - 3 - 4$

   e $10 + 4 - 5$ **f** $10 - 5 + 4$ **g** $18 + 8 - 2$ **h** $18 - 2 + 8$

6 Following the priority of operations, work out

   a $2 \times 3 + 4$ **b** $4 \times 2 + 3$ **c** $2 + 3 \times 4$ **d** $3 + 2 \times 4$

   e $10 \times 2 - 4$ **f** $10 - 2 \times 4$ **g** $12 \div 4 - 2$ **h** $12 - 4 \div 2$

> **Reflect**   Why do you think it is important to have a rule for which operation to calculate first?
> Calculate $10 \times 3 - 2$ by doing the multiplication first. Then calculate it again doing the
> subtraction first. What do you notice?

2.2 Addition and subtraction

- Use a written method to add and subtract whole numbers
- Round whole numbers to the nearest 10, 100 and 1000

Rounding to the nearest 10, 100 and 1000

1 Use the number lines to round these numbers.

   a i 46 to the nearest 10

      ii 42 to the nearest 10

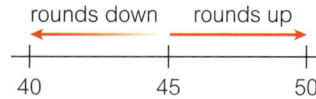

   b i 127 to the nearest 100

      ii 169 to the nearest 100

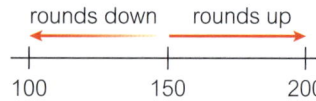

   c i 7011 to the nearest 1000

      ii 7804 to the nearest 1000

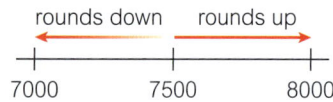

2 Use the number lines to round these numbers.

   a 65 to the nearest 10

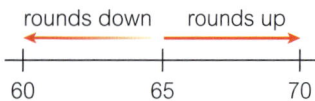

   b 450 to the nearest 100

   c 1500 to the nearest 1000

   d 5500 to the nearest 1000

> **Q2 hint** When the number is exactly halfway you round up.

Addition

Worked example

Work out 35 + 23.

35 + 23

30 + 5 + 20 + 3   — Split the numbers into tens and ones.

30 + 20 + 5 + 3   — Group together the tens and ones. Add the tens, then add the ones.

50 + 8   — Now add together the two answers.

58

1 Copy and complete.

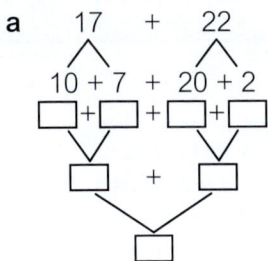

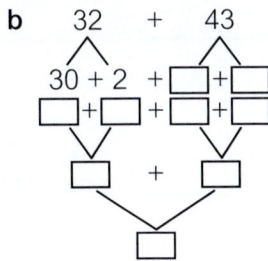

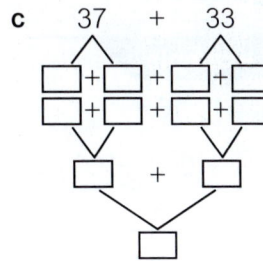

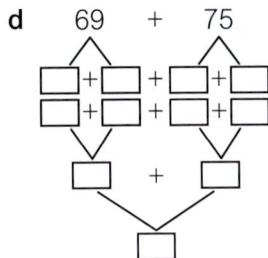

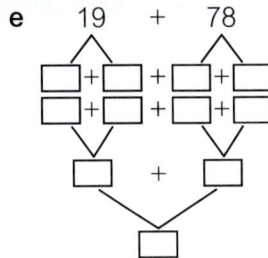

a   17   +   22
10 + 7 + 20 + 2
□+□ + □+□
□   +   □
□

b   32   +   43
30 + 2 + □+□
□+□ + □+□
□   +   □
□

c   37   +   33
□+□ + □+□
□+□ + □+□
□   +   □
□

d   69   +   75
□+□ + □+□
□+□ + □+□
□   +   □
□

e   19   +   78
□+□ + □+□
□+□ + □+□
□   +   □
□

2 Write down the number you need to add to make 100.

a 26
b 78
c 3
d 39
e 94

> **Q2a hint** Draw a number line to help you. Count to the nearest tens number. Then count up to 100 in tens.
>
> +4   +70
>
> 26   30   100

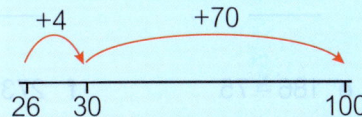

3 Copy and complete these calculations using the column method.

a   8 5
    + 1 3
    ─────
     □ 8

b   7 2
    + 2 1
    ─────
     □□

c   1 2 6
    + 3 3
    ─────
     □□□

4 Copy and complete these calculations.

a i 7 + 6 = □ tens and 3 ones

   ii   1 2 7
        + 2 3 6
        ───────
         □□ 3
           1

b i 8 + 7 = □ tens and □ ones

   ii   3 0 8
        + 1 5 7
        ───────
         □□□

5 Copy and complete these calculations.

a   1 7 6
    + 6 5 2
    ───────
     □ 2 □
       1

b   9 3 5
    + 4 5 1
    ───────
     □□□

> **Q5a hint** 70 + 50 = □ hundreds and □ tens

2.5 Money and time

* Round money to the nearest whole pound or penny
* Solve problems involving money and time

Working with money

Key point   50p = £0.50   5p = £0.05

1 Copy and complete. The first one has been done for you.

a 50p = £0.50   **b** 5p = £☐   **c** 20p = £☐   **d** 2p = £☐

e 7p = £☐   **f** 70p = £☐   **g** 3p = £☐   **h** 30p = £☐

2 Match each price in pence to the price in pounds and pence.

3 Three DVDs cost different amounts.

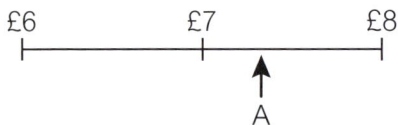

A	B	C
£7.35	£6.99	£6.58

a Copy the number line and show the price of each DVD on the number line. The first one has been done for you.

£6   £7   £8

A

b Use the number line to help you round the cost of each DVD to the nearest pound.

Key point   When the value is exactly halfway between two whole numbers, round up. For example, £4.50 rounded to the nearest pound is £5.

4 Use the number line to help you round the amounts to the nearest pound.

round up

£3   £3.10   £3.20   £3.30   £3.40   £3.50   £3.60   £3.70   £3.80   £3.90   £4

a £3.05   **b** £3.19   **c** £3.35   **d** £3.42

e £3.50   **f** £3.64   **g** £3.76   **h** £3.99

5 Draw your own number line to help you round these amounts to the nearest pound.

    a £7.94   **b** £5.05   **c** £7.23   **d** £14.81

Working with time

1 Write how many minutes there are in

    a 1 hour   **b** 2 hours   **c** 3 hours   **d** 10 hours

---

Worked example

a Write 3 hours and 15 minutes in minutes.

$3 \times 60 = 180$ — Work out how many minutes there are in 3 hours.

$180 + 15 = 195$

3 hours 15 minutes = 195 minutes — Add on the minutes.

b Write 100 minutes in hours and minutes.

$100 \div 60 = 1$ remainder 40 — Work out how many whole hours there are by dividing by 60. The remainder will be the minutes.

100 minutes = 1 hour 40 minutes

---

2 Write these times in minutes.

    a 2 hour 10 minutes   **b** 5 hours 45 minutes   **c** 4 hours 18 minutes

3 Write these times in hours and minutes.

    a 150 minutes   **b** 200 minutes   **c** 312 minutes

4 Copy and complete. The first one has been done for you.

    a $\frac{1}{2}$ hour $= \frac{1}{2} \times 60 = 30$ minutes   **b** $\frac{1}{4}$ hour $= \frac{1}{4} \times 60 = \square$ minutes

    c $\frac{3}{4}$ hour $= \frac{3}{4} \times \square = \square$ minutes   **d** 0.1 hour $= 0.1 \times 60 = \square$ minutes

    e 0.6 hour $= 0.6 \times \square = \square$ minutes   **f** 0.25 hour $= 0.25 \times \square = \square$ minutes

    g 0.5 hour $= 0.5 \times \square = \square$ minutes   **h** 0.75 hour $= 0.75 \times \square = \square$ minutes

5 Which of these statements are true?

    a $\frac{1}{2}$ hour $= 0.5$ hour   **b** $\frac{1}{2}$ hour $= 50$ minutes

    c $\frac{1}{4}$ hour $= 0.4$ hour   **d** 1.5 hours $= 150$ minutes

    e 2.5 hours $= 150$ minutes   **f** 3.25 hours $= 325$ minutes

---

Reflect   When you enter time and money into a calculator you need to enter it in decimal form.

Explain why 3 hours and 40 minutes is not the same as 3.4 hours.

2.6 Negative numbers

- Order positive and negative numbers
- Add and subtract positive and negative numbers

Ordering positive and negative numbers

1 Write these numbers in order from smallest to largest.

11   71   19   3   45   64   123

2 Look at the thermometer on the right.
  a Write the temperatures marked A to E.
  b Which is the highest temperature?
  c Which is the lowest temperature?

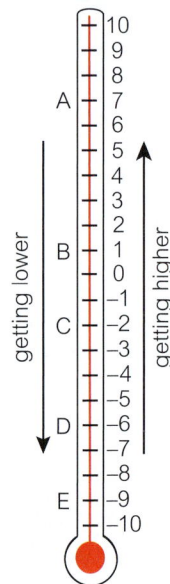

> **Key point** > means greater than. < means less than.

3 a Copy and underline the higher temperature.
  i 1°C   7°C
  ii 1°C   −6°C
  iii −2°C   −6°C
  iv −9°C   −2°C
  b Write > or < between each pair of temperatures in part **a**.

> **Q3b hint** Higher temperature > lower temperature or lower temperature < higher temperature

4 The temperature is recorded in three countries:

Iceland	England	Norway
−20°C	3°C	−5°C

  a Write the country that is
  i coldest
  ii warmest
  b Write the numbers −20, 3 and −5 in order from smallest to largest.

> **Q4b hint** The smallest is always the negative with the highest number.

5 Write these lists of numbers in size order from smallest to largest.
  a −3, −5, 4
  b 1, −1, 2, −3
  c 6, −5, 4, 10, −8
  d −8, −2, 1, −4, −9

(thermometer scale) getting lower ← 10 9 8 7 6 5 4 3 2 1 0 −1 −2 −3 −4 −5 −6 −7 −8 −9 −10 → getting higher
A at 7, B at 1, C at −2, D at −6, E at −9

6 Use number lines to work out

a 1 + 5

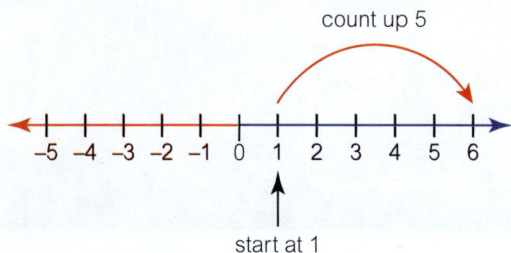

count up 5

start at 1

b −1 + 5

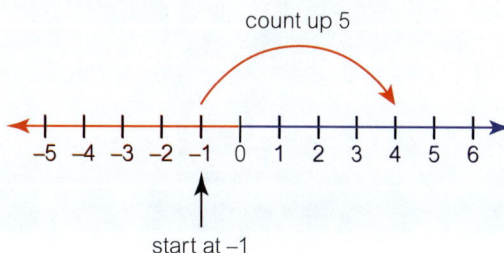

count up 5

start at −1

c −2 + 5   **d** −4 + 5   **e** −5 + 5

7 Use a number line to work out

a −2 + 6	**b** −2 + 7	**c** −2 + 8	**d** −1 + 6
e −1 + 7	**f** −1 + 8	**g** −8 + 2	**h** −8 + 4
i −8 + 8	**j** −11 + 3	**k** −11 + 6	**l** −11 + 12

Subtraction calculations that give negative answers

Worked example

Work out 8 − 12

Draw a number line. Mark the starting point at 8.

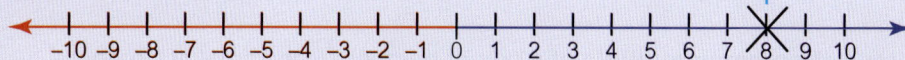

To subtract 12, count down 12 along the number line.

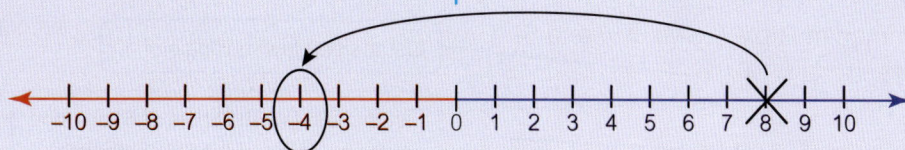

8 − 12 = −4

1 Use a number line to work out

a 10 − 12	**b** 10 − 13	**c** 10 − 14	**d** 4 − 8
e 4 − 10	**f** 4 − 12	**g** 11 − 12	**h** 11 − 15
i 11 − 17	**j** 9 − 13	**k** 3 − 9	**l** 8 − 17

2 Work out

a −1 − 3	**b** −2 − 3	**c** −4 − 2
d −3 − 5	**e** −1 − 5	

Q2a hint Use a number line. Start at −1 and count down 3.

Reflect   Work out 5 − 8.

Write down **five** other calculations that give the same answer. Compare them with a partner.

Do the same for −2 − 5.

Factors, multiples and primes

- Work out multiples and find the lowest common multiple
- Find all factor pairs of a number and the highest common factor of two numbers
- Recognise prime numbers

Multiples

Key point A **multiple** of a number is in that number's multiplication table. For example, the multiples of 7 are: $1 \times 7 = \mathbf{7}$, $2 \times 7 = \mathbf{14}$, $3 \times 7 = \mathbf{21}$, $4 \times 7 = \mathbf{28}$, $5 \times 7 = \mathbf{35}$, ... (You could go on writing down multiples of 7 forever!)

1   Write the first five multiples of
    a 3   **b** 4   **c** 6   **d** 8

2   **a** List all the multiples of 2 that are less than 20.
    b List all the multiples of 5 that are less than 20.
    c Circle the common multiples of 2 and 5 in your lists.

    Q2c hint The common multiples of 2 and 5 are in **both** your lists.

Key point The **lowest common multiple** of a pair of numbers is the smallest integer that is a multiple of **both** the numbers.

Worked example

Find the lowest common multiple (LCM) of 4 and 6.
Multiples of 4: 4, 8, 12, 16, 20, 24, ...

List the first few multiples of 4.

Multiples of 6: 6, 12, ...

List the first few multiples of 6, but stop when you find a number in both lists.

LCM = 12

The LCM is the first multiple that is in **both** lists.

3   **a** List the first eight multiples of 3.
    b List the multiples of 5 until you find a number that is in the list of multiples of 3.
    c What is the LCM of 3 and 5?

4   The first five multiples of 10, 15 and 20 are listed.
    Multiples of 10: 10, 20, 30, 40, 50
    Multiples of 15: 15, 30, 45, 60, 75
    Multiples of 20: 20, 40, 60, 80, 100
    Write the LCM of
    a 10 and 15   **b** 10 and 20   **c** 15 and 20

5 a Copy and complete the table.

Number	First 10 multiples
5	5, 10, 15, 20, 25, 30, 35, 40, 45, 50
6	
7	
8	

b Use the table to find the LCM of

   i 5 and 6   **ii** 5 and 7   **iii** 5 and 8

   iv 6 and 7   **v** 6 and 8   **vi** 7 and 8

Factors

> **Key point**   A **factor** is a whole number that divides exactly into another number.
> For example, 4 divides exactly into 20.
> A factor pair is two numbers that multiply together to make a number. For example, 4 and 5
> are a factor pair of 20.

1 Follow these steps to find **all** the factors of 12. Write the missing number for each multiplication.

   a Is 1 a factor? $1 \times \square = 12$

     So 1 and 12 are a factor pair.

   b Is 2 a factor? $2 \times \square = 12$

     So 2 and $\square$ are a factor pair.

   c Is 3 a factor? $3 \times \square = 12$

     So 3 and $\square$ are a factor pair.

   d Is 5 a factor?

   e You have already found that 6 is a factor. Are there any more factors of 12?

   f Write the factors in order from smallest to largest.

2 Find all the factors of

   a 15   **b** 18   **c** 25   **d** 24

> **Key point**   The **highest common factor** of a pair of numbers is the greatest integer that
> will divide into **both** of the numbers leaving no remainder.

Worked example

a Find the common factors of 12 and 18.

Factors of 12: ①, ②, ③, 4, ⑥ 12

Factors of 18: ①, ②, ③, ⑥ 9, 18

Common factors are: 1, 2, 3, 6

                                           List all the factors of 12 and 18.
Circle the factors in both lists.

b Find the highest common factor (HCF) of 12 and 18.   The HCF is the greatest number
that appears in **both** lists.

HCF = 6

3 **a** List the factors of 15 and 25, from **Q2**.

  b Circle the common factors of 15 and 25.

  c Find the HCF of 15 and 25.

Guided

4 **a** Copy and complete the table. It has been started for you.

Number	Factors
16	1, 2, 4, 8, 16
20	
24	
28	
30	

  b Write the HCF of

i 16 and 20	**ii** 16 and 24	**iii** 16 and 28	**iv** 16 and 30
v 20 and 24	**vi** 20 and 28	**vii** 20 and 30	**viii** 24 and 28

Primes

Key point   A prime number has **exactly** two factors: itself and 1.
(1 is **not** a prime because it has only one factor.)

Guided

1 **a** Copy and compete this table. It has been started for you.

Number	Factors	Number of factors
1	1	1
2	1, 2	2
3		
4	1, 2, 4	3
5		
6		
7		
8		
9		
10		
11		
12		

  b Which numbers have **exactly** two factors?

  c List the prime numbers less than 12.

Reflect   Are these statements true or false?

a 15 is a prime number as the only factors are 3 and 5.

b There are no even prime numbers.

c 1 is a factor of every number.

d 9 is a factor of 3.

2.8 Square numbers

- Recognise square numbers
- Use a calculator to find squares and square roots
- Use the priority of operations, including powers

Recognising square numbers

Key point **Square numbers** make a square pattern of dots.

1 a Which of these patterns show a square of dots?

   A   B   C

         (pattern C)

   Q1a hint The number of rows will equal the number of columns.

   b Which of 9, 12 and 16 are square numbers?

Key point You get a square number when you multiply a number by itself.
For example, $5 \times 5 = 25$ so 25 is a square number.
You can write 5×5 as 5^2. So $5^2 = 5 \times 5 = 25$

2 a Copy and complete.

   $1^2 = 1 \times 1 = 1$
   $2^2 = 2 \times 2 = \square$
   $3^2 = \square \times \square = \square$
   $4^2 = \square \times \square = \square$
   $5^2 = \square \times \square = \square$

   b Continue the pattern until you have found all the square numbers smaller than 100.
   c How many square numbers are smaller than 100?

Key point You can use a calculator to square a number.
The square key will look like this. $\boxed{x^2}$

3 Use a calculator to work out
   a 18^2 b 25^2 c 91^2 d 108^2 e 213^2

4 **Reasoning** Terri says: 'Squaring is the same as multiplying by 2.'
   Explain why she is wrong.

   Q4 hint You could use a number example to show how it is incorrect.

Square roots

1   **Reasoning**   Harry makes square numbers using tiles.

Harry uses 16 tiles to make the next shape in the sequence.

a How many rows of tiles will he use? How many columns?

b How many rows and columns will be in the next square after that?

2   Write the number that when multiplied by itself makes

a 4   b 36   c 100

> **Key point**   The **square root** of a number is a number that is multiplied by itself to give that number.
> The sign $\sqrt{}$ means square root.
> For example: $10 \times 10 = 100$, so $\sqrt{100} = 10$

3   Work out

a $\sqrt{1}$ b $\sqrt{9}$ c $\sqrt{25}$ d $\sqrt{49}$ e $\sqrt{121}$

> **Key point**   The square root key on your calculator will look something like this: $\boxed{\sqrt{}}$

4   Use a calculator to find the square root of each number.

a $\sqrt{400}$ b $\sqrt{169}$ c $\sqrt{324}$ d $\sqrt{625}$

Powers in priority of operations

> **Key point**   You must use the priority of operations to carry out calculations.
> Use BIDMAS.
> • Brackets
> • Indices (powers) ———— Work out squares (power of 2) before ÷, ×, + or −
> • Division and Multiplication
> • Addition and Subtraction

Guided

1   Copy and complete:

a $3^2 + 2 = 9 + 2 = \square$

b $4 + 5^2 = 4 + \square = \square$

c $3^2 - 5 = \square - 5 = \square$

d $2 \times 4^2 = 2 \times \square = \square$

e $6^2 \div 2 = \square \div 2 = \square$

f $10 - 2^2 = 10 - \square = \square$

> **Reflect**   Erin says: 'The square root of 9 is 81. 9^2 is 3.'
> Explain her mistakes. How should she work out $\sqrt{9}$ and 9^2?

3 Expressions, functions and formulae

3.1 Functions

- Find outputs of simple functions written in words and using symbols

One-step function machines

Worked example

Work out the output of this function machine.

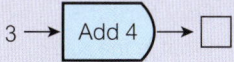

Input → Add 4 → Output □ — The 'rule' or 'function' in this function machine is 'Add 4'.

3 + 4 = 7

Key point   A function or rule is a relationship between two sets of numbers.
The numbers that go into a function machine are called the **inputs**.
The numbers that come out are called the **outputs**.
In a function machine, every input gives an output.

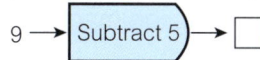

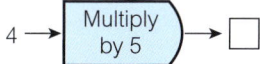

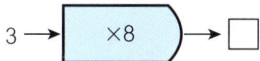

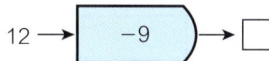

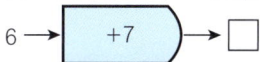

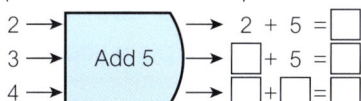

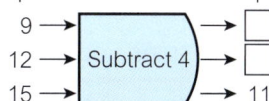

1 Work out the outputs of these function machines.

   a Input 6 → Add 3 → Output □
   b Input 9 → Subtract 5 → Output □
   c Input 4 → Multiply by 5 → Output □
   d Input 16 → Divide by 2 → Output □

   Q1a hint 6 + 3 =

2 Work out the outputs of these function machines.

   a Input 3 → ×8 → Output □
   b Input 12 → −9 → Output □
   c Input 6 → +7 → Output □
   d Input 35 → ÷5 → Output □

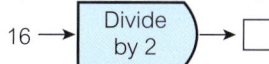

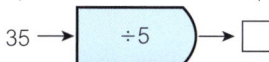

   Q2a hint 3 × 8 =

3 Work out the outputs of these function machines. The first one has been started for you.

   a Input 2 → Add 5 → Output 2 + 5 = □
        3 →   → □ + 5 = □
        4 →   → □ + □ = □
   b Input 9 → Subtract 4 → Output □
        12 →   → □
        15 →   → 11

Guided

4 Work out the outputs of these function machines.

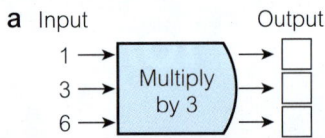

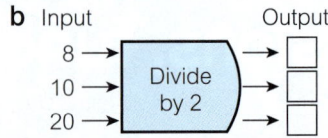

Write the missing rule for this function machine.

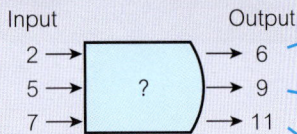

$2 \square = 6$ The rule could be: $2 + 4 = 6$ or $2 \times 3 = 6$

Rule + 4: $5 + 4 = 9$ Rule × 3: $5 \times 3 = 15$
The rule must work for *all* inputs and outputs.

Rule + 4: $7 + 4 = 11$ Rule × 3: $7 \times 3 = 21$

The rule is + 4.

5 Write the rule for each function machine.

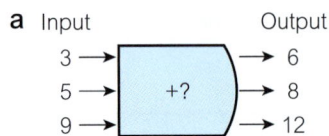

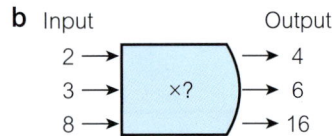

Q5a hint $3 + \square = 6$
What is the rule?
Check your rule
works for all inputs
and outputs.

6 Reasoning

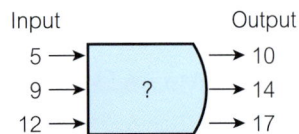

Q6b hint Which of
your rules in **Q6a**
works for *all* inputs
and outputs of this
function machine?

a Write two possible rules for $5 \square = 10$

b Write the rule for this function machine.

Two-step function machines

1 Copy and complete.

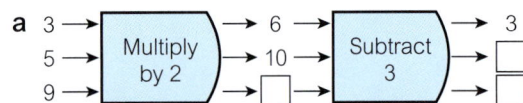

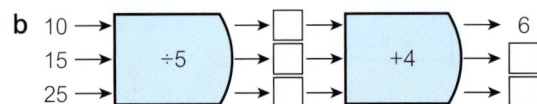

Copy and create four different function machines with four different rules. Use +, −, × and ÷.
Bella says: 'There are only four rules you can write.' Is Bella correct? Explain your reasons.

3.2 Simplifying expressions 1

- Use letters to represent unknowns in algebraic expressions
- Simplify linear algebraic expressions by collecting like terms

Simplifying expressions by adding or subtracting like terms

> **Key point** In maths, if you do not know a value, you can use a letter to represent it.
> The letter is called a **variable**.
> **Terms** can be numbers or a number multiplied by a variable (letter).
> Here are some terms: p $2p$ x $3x$ 5
> **Like terms** have the **same letter**: p and $2p$ are like terms; $2p$ and $2x$ are not.
> You can simplify by collecting (adding or subtracting) like terms.

Worked example

a Simplify $p + p$.

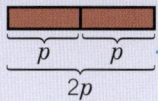

p and p are like terms that can be collected together.

2p

$p + p = 2p$

b Simplify $2p + p$.

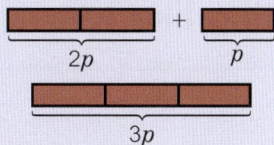

$2p$ and p are like terms that can be collected together.

3p

$2p + p = 3p$

> **Key point** $1x$ is written as x.

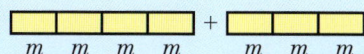

Guided

1 Simplify

  a $x + x$ ☐ + ☐

  b $x + x + x$ ☐ + ☐ + ☐

  c $2x + x$ ☐ + ☐

  d $3x + x$ ☐ + ☐

  e $2x + 2x$ ☐ + ☐

  f $2x + 3x$ ☐ + ☐

2 Simplify

  a $m + m$

  b $m + m + m$

  c $4m + 3m$

  d $4m + 3m + 2m$

> **Q2c hint** ☐☐☐☐ + ☐☐☐
> m m m m m m m

Worked example

Simplify $7y - 2y$.

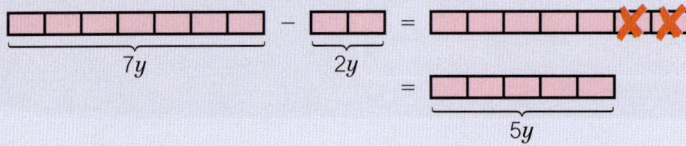

$7y - 2y = 5y$

Guided

3 Simplify

a $5y - 2y$

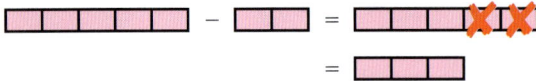

b $7y - 3y$

c $5y - y - 2y$

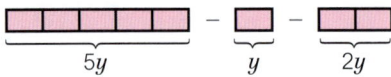

Q3b hint Draw bars to help you.

4 **Reasoning** Mariam says that $3x - x = 3$.

Ena says that $3x - x = 2x$.

Who is correct? Explain your reasons.

Simplifying expressions by adding and subtracting like terms

Worked example

Simplify $3b + 2b - b$. — Work from left to right. First work out $3b + 2b$.

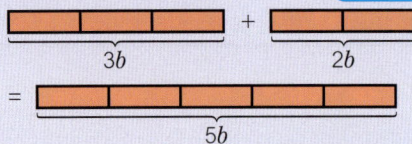

$3b + 2b = 5b$ — Now simplify $5b - b$.

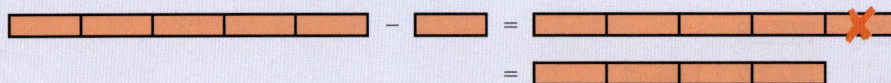

Now subtract b.

$5b - b = 4b$

1 Simplify

a $4m + 2m - m$

b $m + 3m - m$

c $4m + 3m - 2m$

d $4x + 3x - 2x$

35

Simplifying expressions involving variables and numbers

1 Group the like terms.

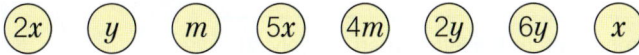

$2x$ y m $5x$ $4m$ $2y$ $6y$ x

2 Simplify

    a $3x + 4x$

    b $3x + 4x + 2$

    c $3x + 4x + y$

    d $3x + 4x + y + 2y$

    e $7y + 2y - 4y$

    f $4x + 2x - 3x$

    g $5p + 4p - p$

> **Q2b hint** $3x + 4x + 2 = \square x + 2$

> **Q2c hint** x terms and y terms are not like terms. $3x + 4x + y = \square x + y$

> **Q2d hint** Work out $3x + 4x$, then work out $y + 2y$.

Guided

3 Rearrange these expressions so that like terms are collected together.

    a $x + y + 2x = x + 2x + \square$

    b $2x + 3y + 3x = 2x + \square x + \square y$

    c $3p + 5t + p = \square p + p + \square t$

    d $4m + 2n - 3m = \square m - \square m + \square n$

> **Q3a hint** $\boxed{x} + \boxed{y} + \boxed{x}\,\boxed{x} =$
> $\boxed{x} + \boxed{x}\,\boxed{x} + \boxed{y}$

Guided

4 Rearrange these expressions so that like terms are collected together.
Simplify these expressions.

    a $4x + 2y - 2x = 4x - 2x + 2y$

                $= \square x + \square y$

    b $5x + 3y - 2x = 5x - \square x + 3y$

                $= \square x + \square y$

    c $3p + 4t - 2p$

    d $4m + 3n - m$

> **Q4a hint** $\boxed{x}\,\boxed{x}\,\boxed{x}\,\boxed{x} + \boxed{y}\,\boxed{y} - \boxed{x}\,\boxed{x} =$
> $\boxed{x}\,\boxed{x}\,\cancel{\boxed{x}}\,\cancel{\boxed{x}} + \boxed{y}\,\boxed{y}$

Reflect   Sanjay simplifies $10a + 5 - 4a - 2$.

He writes the answer $9a$.

What mistake has Sanjay made?

3.3 Simplifying expressions 2

- Multiply and divide algebraic terms
- Use brackets with numbers and letters

Multiplying algebraic terms

Worked example

a Simplify $3 \times x$. —— Write the number before the letter when multiplying.

$3x$

b Simplify $a \times b$. —— $a \times b$ is the same as $b \times a$. We usually write the letters in alphabetical order.

ab

1 Simplify

    a $4 \times y$ **b** $7 \times t$ **c** $a \times 6$ **d** $f \times 10$

2 Simplify

    a $p \times q$ **b** $m \times n$ **c** $b \times a$

Worked example

a Simplify $3y \times 2$. —— You can use a bar model to help.

$3y \times 2 = 3y + 3y$

| y | y | y | | y | y | y |

$6y$

b Simplify $\frac{6y}{2}$

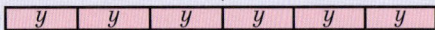

| y | y | y | y | y | y |

$3y$

3 Simplify

    a $2b \times 3$ **b** $4y \times 3$ **c** $2p \times 5$

    d $4 \times 2b$ **e** $6 \times 3a$ **f** $9 \times 2a$

> **Q3d hint** This is the same as $2b \times 4$ because multiplication can be done in any order.

4 Simplify

    a $\frac{8x}{2}$ **b** $\frac{4x}{2}$ **c** $\frac{10x}{2}$

> **Q4a hint** $\frac{8x}{2}$ means $8x \div 2$

Working with brackets

> **Key point** To multiply out (expand) expressions with brackets, multiply all the terms inside the bracket by the term outside the bracket.
> $4(3 + 2)$ is the same as $4 \times (3 + 2)$.

Worked example

Expand $2(30 + 4)$

Draw lines to show which numbers to multiply together.

$2(30 + 4)$

$= 2 \times 30 \ + \ 2 \times 4$

$= 60 + 8 = 68$

×	30	4
2	60	8

$2(30 + 4)$ is equivalent to $2 \times 30 + 2 \times 4$

1 Copy and complete

a $3(20 + 7)$

$= 3 \times 20 + 3 \times \square$

$= \square + \square = \square$

×	20	7
3		

b $4 \times (30 + 2)$

$= 4 \times \square + 4 \times \square$

$= \square + \square = \square$

×	$\square$	$\square$
$\square$		

2 Write each calculation as a simpler calculation using brackets. Then work out the answer. The first one has been started for you.

a $5 \times 23 = 5(20 + 3)$

$= 5 \times \square + \square \times \square = \square$

×	20	3
5		

b 4×53

c 3×26

3 Work out these calculations. The first one has been started for you.

a $2 \times (30 - 3) = \square - 6 = \square$

b $4 \times (20 - 3) = \square - \square = \square$

Q3a hint

×	30	−3
2	60	−6

4 Write each calculation as a simpler calculation using brackets. Then work out the answer. The first one has been started for you.

a $4 \times 59 = 4(60 - 1) = \square - \square = \square$

b 3×58 **c** 2×78

Worked example

Expand and simplify $2(a + 4)$

Draw lines to show which numbers to multiply.

$2(a + 4)$

$2a + 8$

×	a	4
2	$2a$	8

$2(a + 4)$ is equivalent to $2 \times a + 2 \times 4$

5 Expand and simplify

a $4(a + 5)$ **b** $3(a - 2)$

Q5b hint

×	a	−2
3	$\square$	$\square$

Reflect Mark simplifies $2(x - 3)$. He writes the answer $2x + 3$.

What mistake(s) has Mark made? What is the correct answer?

3.4 Writing expressions

- Write expressions from word descriptions using addition, subtraction, multiplication and division
- Write expressions to represent function machines

Writing expressions from word descriptions

1 There are 20 counters in a bag. Write an expression for
- **a** the number of counters in the bag when 4 counters are added
- **b** the number of counters in the bag when 2 counters are taken away
- **c** the number of counters in 3 bags

Worked example

Claire has a bag containing n counters.

> Letters are used to represent unknown numbers (variables).

Write an expression for
- **a** the number of counters in the bag when 4 counters are added
$n + 4$
- **b** the number of counters in the bag when 2 counters are taken away
$n - 2$
- **c** the number of counters in 3 bags
$3 \times n = 3n$

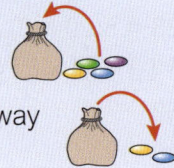

Key point An expression does not contain an equals sign.

2 There are c sweets in a bag.
Write an expression for
- **a** the number of sweets in the bag when 5 sweets are added
- **b** the number of sweets in the bag when 3 sweets are taken out
- **c** the number of sweets in 7 bags

Q2a hint $c + \square$

3 **Problem-solving** Joe is a years old.
Write an expression for the age of each of these people.
- **a** Mike, who is 4 years older than Joe.
- **b** Hadia, who is 10 years older than Joe.
- **c** Sarah, who is 6 years younger than Joe.
- **d** Chen, who is 4 years younger than Joe.
- **e** Larry, who is twice the age of Joe.

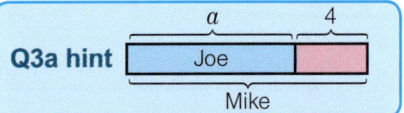

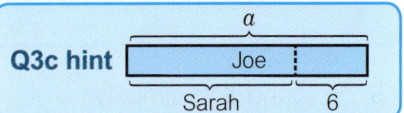

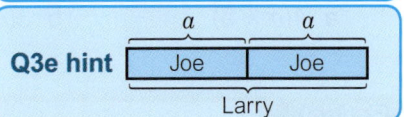

4 Problem-solving The length of a rod is x cm. Write an expression for the length of

a a rod that is 4 cm longer than x

b 3 rods

c 6 rods

Q4b hint

x x x

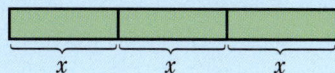

Writing expressions using function machines

Worked example

a Draw a function machine to write an expression for 7 more than x.

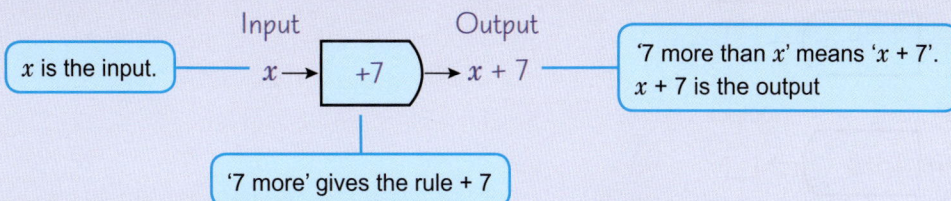

Input   Output

x is the input. $x \rightarrow$ [+7] $\rightarrow x + 7$ '7 more than x' means '$x + 7$'. $x + 7$ is the output

'7 more' gives the rule + 7

b Use the same function machine to work out the output when $x = 3$.

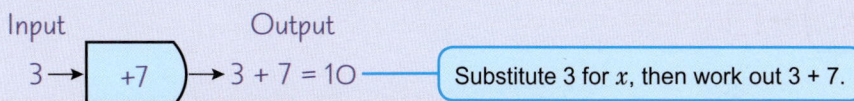

Input   Output

$3 \rightarrow$ [+7] $\rightarrow 3 + 7 = 10$ Substitute 3 for x, then work out 3 + 7.

1 a i Copy and complete this function machine to write an expression for 5 more than y.

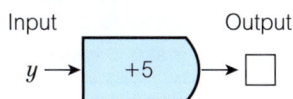

Input   Output

$y \rightarrow$ [+5] $\rightarrow \square$

ii Use the function machine to work out the output when $y = 11$.

b i Copy and complete this function machine to write an expression for 6 less than m.

Input   Output

$m \rightarrow$ [−6] $\rightarrow \square$

ii Use the function machine to work out the output when $m = 15$

c i Copy and complete this function machine to write an expression for 5 times p.

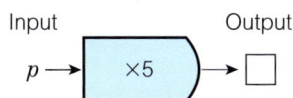

Input   Output

$p \rightarrow$ [×5] $\rightarrow \square$

Q1ci hint Write numbers before letters when multiplying.

ii Use the function machine to work out the output when $p = 3$

d i Copy and complete this function machine to write an expression for one quarter of z.

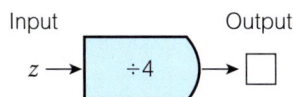

Input   Output

$z \rightarrow$ [÷4] $\rightarrow \square$

Q1di hint Write the letter over the number: $\frac{z}{\square}$

ii Use the function machine to work out the output when $z = 8$.

2 **Problem-solving** Match each expression to one of the four function machines.

    a double n

    b 2 subtracted from n

    c half n

    d 2 added to n.

> **Q2a hint** When you double a number, do you add, subtract, multiply or divide?

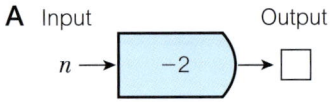

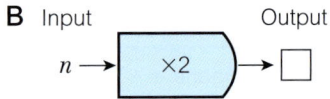

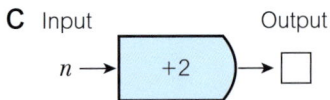

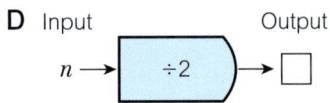

A Input   Output

    $n \rightarrow$ [−2] → ☐

B Input   Output

    $n \rightarrow$ [×2] → ☐

C Input   Output

    $n \rightarrow$ [+2] → ☐

D Input   Output

    $n \rightarrow$ [÷2] → ☐

3 **Problem-solving** Dave earns £a each week.

Match a function machine to each of his friends.

    a Petra earns £3 less than Dave each week.

    b Crista earns 3 times as much as Dave each week.

    c Jameel earns £3 more than Dave each week.

    d Pete works part-time. He earns one third of the amount that Dave earns each week.

> **Q3a hint** Which function machine gives an output that is 3 less than a?

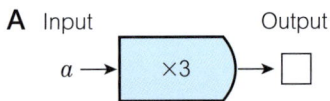

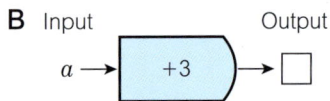

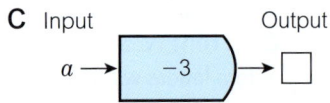

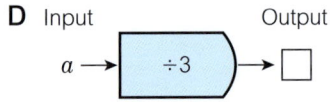

A Input   Output

    $a \rightarrow$ [×3] → ☐

B Input   Output

    $a \rightarrow$ [+3] → ☐

C Input   Output

    $a \rightarrow$ [−3] → ☐

D Input   Output

    $a \rightarrow$ [÷3] → ☐

Reflect   This lesson used bar models and function machines.

Draw a bar model and a function machine to represent each of these expressions.

    a $x + 5$ **b** $5x$

3.5 Substituting into formulae

- Substitute positive whole numbers into simple formulae written in words
- Substitute positive whole numbers into formulae written with letters

Formulae written in words

Key point A **formula** shows the relationship between different quantities.
You can write a formula using words to describe quantities.
A formula always has an equals sign '='.

Worked example

The formula to work out the perimeter of a regular hexagon is:
    perimeter = 6 × length of one side
Work out the perimeter when the length of one side is 5 cm.

perimeter = 6 × length of one side ⎯⎯⎯ Write the formula first.
        = 6 × 5
        = 30 cm ⎯⎯⎯ Substitute the value for the length of one side into the formula.

1 **Problem-solving** The formula to work out the perimeter of a regular pentagon is

   perimeter = 5 × length of one side

   Work out the perimeter of a regular pentagon when
   the length of one side is

   Q1a hint perimeter = 5 × 2 = ☐ cm

   a 2 cm   **b** 3 cm   **c** 4 cm   **d** 10 cm

2 **Problem-solving** The formula to work out the distance travelled by a bicycle in 2 hours is

   distance = 2 × speed

   Work out the distance travelled by a bicycle when the speed is

   a 20 km/h   **Q2a hint** distance = 2 × 20 = ☐ km
   b 25 km/h
   c 30 km/h
   d 50 km/h

3 **Problem-solving** The formula to work out the number of people that can be seated at
   small tables in a café is

   people = 4 × number of tables

   Work out how many people can be seated at

   a 6 tables   **Q3a hint** 4 × ☐ = ☐
   b 8 tables
   c 10 tables
   d 20 tables

Using patterns to write formulae in words and letters

Worked example

Sally earns £9 per hour.

a   Write a calculation to work out how much Sally earns in 2 hours.

2 × £9

b   Write a calculation to work out how much Sally earns in 3 hours.

3 × £9

c   Write a formula to connect how much Sally earns, m, to the number of hours, h.

h × £9 ——— Follow the pattern.

$m = h$ × £9 ——— Write as a formula with an = sign.

$m = £9h$ ——— Rearrange and simplify the formula.

Guided

1   **Problem-solving**   Casimir buys some pens. Each pen costs £2.

    a   Copy and complete this formula in words for the total cost of 2 pens.

       total cost = 2 pens × ☐

    b   Copy and complete this formula in words for the total cost of 3 pens.

       total cost = 3 pens × ☐

    c   Look at the pattern. Write a formula to connect the total cost, c, to the number of pens, p.

       $c = ☐ × ☐ = ☐$

Guided

2   a   **Problem-solving**   Joe is making burgers. For each burger he needs two cheese slices.

      i   Complete this formula in words for the number of cheese slices Joe will need for 5 burgers.

        number of cheese slices = 5 × ☐

      ii   Complete this formula in words for the number of cheese slices Joe will need for 10 burgers.

        number of cheese slices = 10 × ☐

      iii   Look at the pattern. Write a formula to connect the number of cheese slices, n, to the number of burgers, b.

        $n = ☐ × ☐ = ☐$

    b   Write a calculation to work out the number of cheese slices, n, when you know the number of burgers, b.

      i   When $b = 2$ $n = ☐ × ☐ = ☐$

      ii   When $b = 3$ $n = ☐ × ☐ = ☐$

Reflect   In lesson 3.4 you looked at writing expressions. In this lesson you looked at writing formulae.

Discuss with a partner the differences between an expression and a formula.

4 Decimals and measures

4.1 Decimals and rounding

- Measure and draw lines to the nearest millimetre
- Write decimals in order of size
- Round decimals to the nearest whole number

Understanding decimals with tenths

Key point
A **decimal number** has a **decimal point**.
Digits after the decimal point are parts of a whole.

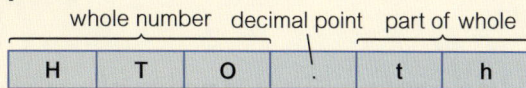

whole number			decimal point	part of whole	
H	T	O	.	t	h

1 State whether or not these are **decimal numbers**.

     a 1.2   **b** 45   **c** 0.4   **d** 3.02

2   **Problem-solving**   Look at these numbers.

     2.1   2.5   5.2   7.5

     a Write the numbers that have the same **whole numbers**.

     b Write the numbers that have the same **parts of a whole**.

Key point

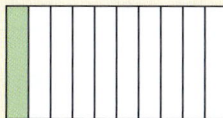

tenths hundredths

H	T	O	.	t	h
		0	.	1	
		0	.	0	1

0.1 means 1 tenth

3 Write the decimal number shown in each diagram.   **Q3 hint** Count the long bars to find the tenths.

   a    **b** 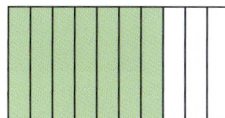   **c**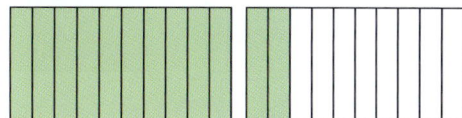

Key point   The **number of digits after the decimal point** is called the number of **decimal places** (or d.p.).

Guided

4 Write the measurement in cm shown by each arrow. Give each measurement to **1 decimal place** (1 d.p.). Part **a** has been done for you.

5 For each line

    i estimate its length by looking and making a guess

    ii measure it accurately using a ruler to the nearest mm

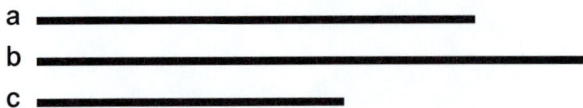

a ▬▬▬▬▬▬▬▬▬▬▬▬▬▬▬▬

b ▬▬▬▬▬▬▬▬▬▬▬▬▬▬▬▬▬▬

c ▬▬▬▬▬▬▬▬▬▬▬▬

Q5 hint Carefully line up the zero marker on your ruler with the start of the line

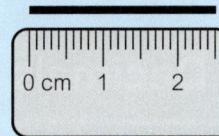

6 Using pencil and a ruler, draw a line with length:

    a 4 cm   **b** 6.3 cm

Q6 hint Hold your ruler steady and draw the line with a pencil.

Mark where your line will go

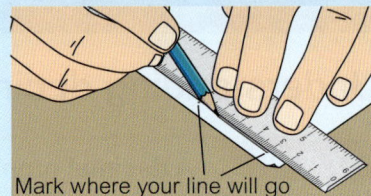

7 **Problem-solving** Which of these numbers are written to 1 decimal place?

    5.25   23.9   1.7   18.46

    8   3.0   76.32   8.8

Understanding decimals with tenths and hundredths

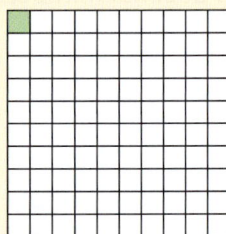

Key point

tenths hundredths

H	T	O	.	t	h
		0	.	1	
		0	.	0	1

0.01 means 1 hundredth

1 Write the decimal number shown in each diagram.

Q1 hint Count the long bars first to find the tenths, then count the small squares to find the hundredths.

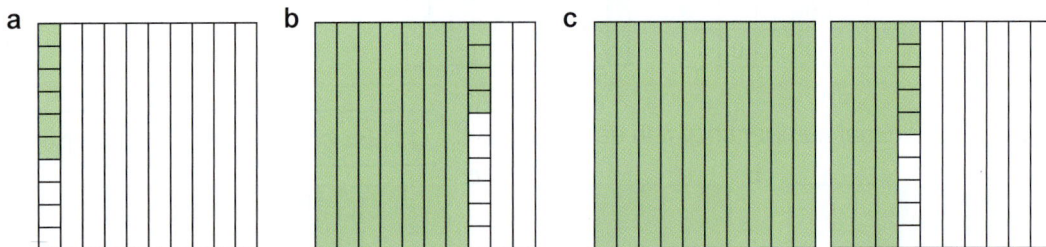

a   **b**   **c**

2 **a** Copy the place value table. Write these numbers in it.

    i 3   **ii** 3.1   **iii** 3.06

    b Write how many

      i tenths are in 3.1   **ii** hundredths are in 3.06

T	O	.	t	h

3 For the decimal numbers

    a 0.4   **b** 0.74   **c** 0.04   **d** 1.41

    i write out the number in words   **ii** write the value of the 4

Q3b hint We say 0.74 as 'zero point seven four'.

Ordering decimals

1 Write the value of the tenths in

Q1d hint 6 is the same as 6.0

    a 3.2   **b** 3.87   **c** 9.04   **d** 6

2 Which decimal number in each pair has more tenths?

    a 0.2 or 0.4   **b** 0.18 or 0.8   **c** 0.73 or 0.08   **d** 0.4 or 0.7

> **Key point** When comparing numbers, we can use **>** for '**greater than**' and **<** for '**less than**', for example: 10 > 2.

3 Write > or < between each pair of numbers.

    a 1.2 ☐ 1.5   **b** 2.4 ☐ 1.5

    c 7.1 ☐ 7.08   **d** 1.14 ☐ 1.2

Q4 hint Compare the ones digits – is one larger or smaller than the other? If both ones digits are the same, check if the tenths digit is larger or smaller.

4 **Problem-solving** Fill in the gaps.

    a 4.4 < 4.☐   **b** 5.1 > 5.☐   **c** 8.7 < ☐

    d Repeat parts **a** to **c** with different answers.

5 Write each set of decimal numbers in order, from smallest to largest.

Q6 hint Start with the smallest ones digit. Then check the tenths digits and then the hundredths digits.

    a 1.2   1.3   1.7   1.1   1.4   **b** 2.32 2.35 2.39 2.31 2.34

    c 8.12 8.03 8.4   8.3   8.31   **d** 7.1   7.04 7.11 7.01 7.09

Rounding decimals

> **Key point**
>
> rounds down   rounds up
>
> ⊢————————⊢————————⊢
> 3.0   3.5   4.0

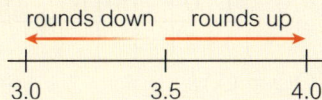

1 Round these measurements to the nearest whole centimetre. Use the ruler to help you.

    a 3.2 cm   **b** 4.8 cm   **c** 6.4 cm

2 For each value indicated by an arrow

Q2 hint The space between each line is 0.1.

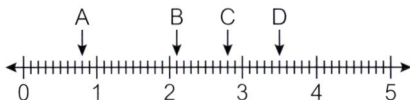

    a write the value   **b** round it to the nearest whole number

3 Round each of these to the nearest whole number.

    a 12.3   **b** 7.8   **c** 4.5

> **Reflect** Discuss these questions with a partner.
>
> **a** Why is 2 the same as 2.0 and 2.00?   **b** Which is larger, 2.02 or 2.20?

4.2 Length, mass and capacity

- Multiply and divide whole numbers and decimals by 10, 100 and 1000
- Convert between metric units of length, mass and capacity

Multiplying and dividing by 10, 100 and 1000

1 Work out

    a 5 × 10   **b** 43 × 10   **c** 76 × 100

Q1 hint ×10

H	T	O
	4	0

÷10

2 Work out

    a 90 ÷ 10   **b** 300 ÷ 10   **c** 600 ÷ 100

Worked example

Work out

a 5.2 × 10   ×10

T	O	.	t
	5	.	2

→

T	O	.	t
5	2	.	

5.2 × 10 = 52

b 4.5 × 100   ×100

H	T	O	.	t
		4	.	5

→

H	T	O	.	t
4	5	0	.	

4.5 × 100 = 450

3 Work out

    a 4.6 × 10   **b** 4.6 × 100   **c** 7.34 × 100   **d** 7.34 × 1000

Worked example

Work out

a 67 ÷ 10   ÷10

T	O	.	t
6	7	.	

→

T	O	.	t
	6	.	7

67 ÷ 10 = 6.7

b 12 ÷ 100   ÷100

T	O	.	t	h
1	2	.		

→

T	O	.	t	h
	0	.	1	2

12 ÷ 100 = 0.12

4 Work out

    a 51 ÷ 10   **b** 51 ÷ 100   **c** 871 ÷ 100   **d** 871 ÷ 1000

Converting measures of length

1 Write how many mm there are in a cm, looking at your ruler to find the answer.

2 **Problem-solving** Choose the most suitable unit of length: mm, cm, m or km to measure

    a the length of the whiteboard   **b** the distance between two towns

    c the width of the school hall   **d** the width of a fingernail

Key point

1 kilometre (km) = 1000 metres (m)
1 metre (m) = 100 centimetres (cm)
1 centimetre (cm) = 10 millimetres (mm)

×1000   ×100   ×10
km   m   cm   mm
÷1000   ÷100   ÷10

Guided

3 Use a double number line to convert between cm and mm.

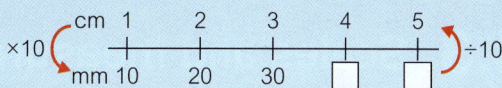

Q3 hint

cm 1   2   3   4   5
×10 ⌒
mm 10 20   30   ☐   ☐ ÷10

   a 2 cm = ☐ × 10 = ☐ mm   **b** 6.5 cm = ☐ mm
   c 40 mm = ☐ ÷ 10 = ☐ cm   **d** 48 mm = ☐ cm

Guided

4 Copy and complete these calculations to convert between cm, m and km.
   a 5 m = 5 × 100 = ☐ cm   **b** 3 m = ☐ cm   **c** 314 cm = 314 ÷ 100 = ☐ m
   d 482 cm = ☐ m   **e** 7 km = 7 × 1000 = ☐ m   **f** 2 km = ☐ m
   g 9200 m = 9200 ÷ 1000 = ☐ km   **h** 2300 m = ☐ km

5 **Problem-solving** Daniel is 1.4 m tall and Anita is 145 cm tall. Who is taller?

Q5 hint Convert to the same units first, then compare.

6 Write these lengths in order, shortest first.
   a 400 cm   3.5 m   345 cm   4.2 m
   b 2.12 m   3 m   234 cm   303 cm

Q6 hint Convert to the same units first, then put in order.

Converting measures of mass and capacity

Key point Mass measures how much something weighs.
1 kilogram (kg) = 1000 grams (g)

Guided

1 Copy and complete these calculations to convert between kg and g.
   a 2.3 kg = 2.3 × 1000 = ☐ g   **b** 4.6 kg = ☐ g
   c 1200 g = 1200 ÷ 1000 = ☐ kg   **d** 6400 g = ☐ kg

Key point Capacity measures the amount a container holds.
1 litre = 1000 millilitres (ml)

2 **Reasoning** Choose the most suitable unit (ml or litres), to measure the capacity of
   a a test tube   **b** a fuel tank   **c** a swimming pool

Guided

3 Copy and complete these calculations to convert between litres and ml.
   a 9.4 litres = 9.4 × 1000 = ☐ ml   **b** 7.5 litres = ☐ ml
   c 7320 ml = 7320 ÷ 1000 = ☐ litres   **d** 2410 ml = ☐

4 **Reasoning** Choose which unit (ml, g or cm), you would use to measure
   a the length of a table   **b** the mass of a bag of sugar   **c** the capacity of a bottle

Reflect Discuss with your partner
   a how to convert from a smaller unit to a larger unit, for example: 450 cm to m
   b how to convert from a larger unit to a smaller unit, for example: 3.7 km to m

4.3 Scales and measures

- Read scales
- Use scale diagrams

Scale drawing

1 Write the measures marked by the arrows in

   a centimetres   b millimetres

Q1 hint There are 10 mm in 1 cm.

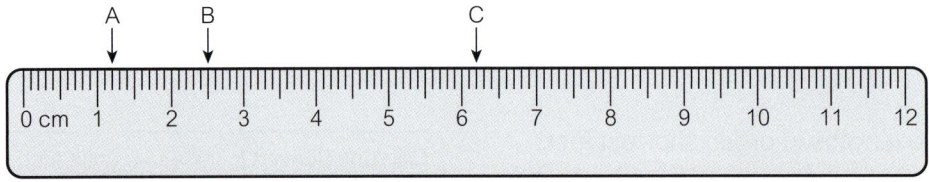

> **Key point**   A **scale drawing** uses a small space to show a large real-life measure.
> It needs a scale to tell you what 1 cm on the drawing represents in real life.

Worked example

This rectangle is on a 1 cm squared grid. 1 cm on the grid represents 1 m in real life.

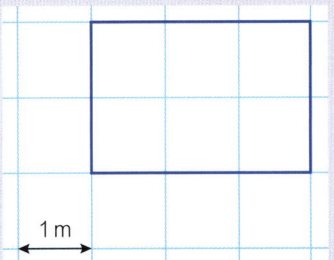

Write the length and the width of the rectangle in metres.

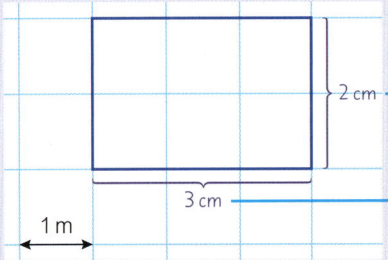

2 cm on the scale drawing is **2 m** in real life.

3 cm on the scale drawing is **3 m** in real life.

Width = 2 m and length = 3 m

2 This diagram is on a 1 cm squared grid. 1 cm on the grid represents 1 m in real life.

   a How long is the line on the scale drawing?

   b How long is the line in real life?

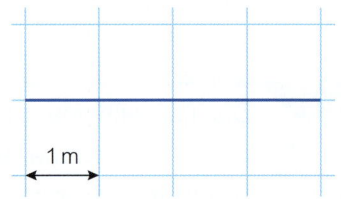

3 This square is on a 1 cm squared grid. 1 cm on the grid represents 1 m in real life.

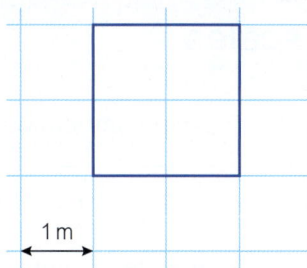

　　a How wide is the square on the scale drawing?

　　b How wide is the square in real life?

Guided

4 On a scale drawing, 1 cm represents 1 m. Draw lines representing these lengths on squared paper. The first one has been done for you.

　a 3 m　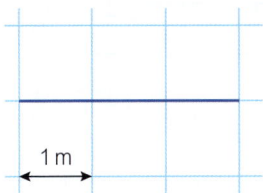　　　**b** 5 m　　　　　　**c** 4.5 m

Reading simple scales counting by 1 or 0.1

1 Write the measurement shown by each arrow.

> **Q1 hint** Remember to write the units.

a 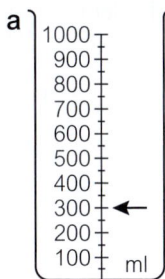　**b** 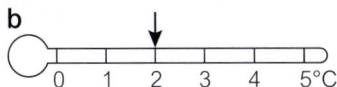　**c**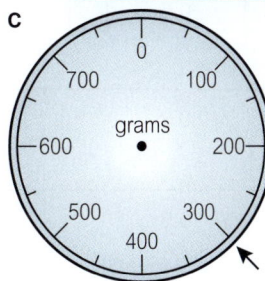

2 Write the measurement shown by each arrow.

> **Q2 hint** Work out what the scale goes up in.

a 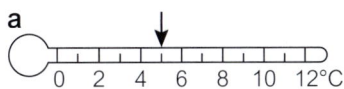　**b** 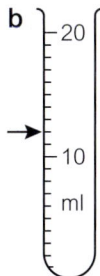　**c**

3 Write the measurements shown on these scales.

a 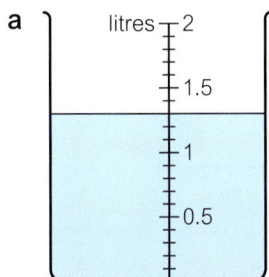　**b**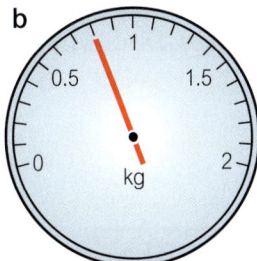

More scales

Q2 hint Work out what the number line goes up in.

1 Fill in the missing numbers on these number lines.

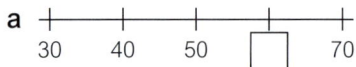

a
```
30   40   50   □   70
```

b
```
200   □   400   500   600
```

2 Copy and complete the number lines.

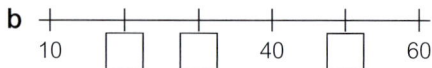

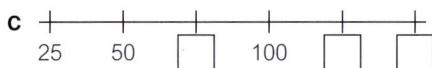

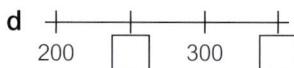

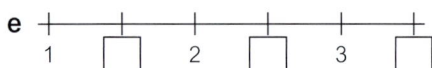

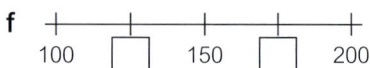

a
```
2   4   □   □   10   □
```

b
```
10   □   □   40   □   60
```

c
```
25   50   □   100   □   □
```

d
```
200   □   300   □
```

e
```
1   □   2   □   3   □
```

f
```
100   □   150   □   200
```

g
```
100   □   200   □   □   300
```

h
```
150   □   □   □   160
```

3 Copy and complete.

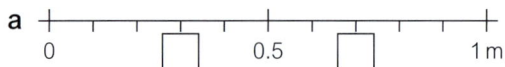

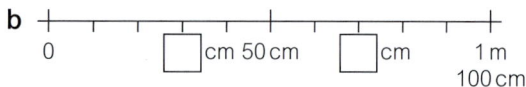

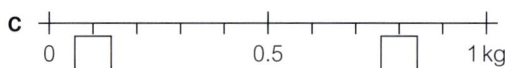

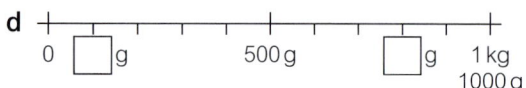

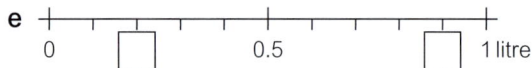

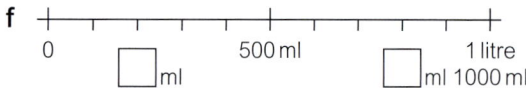

a
```
0   □   0.5   □   1 m
```

b
```
0   □ cm  50 cm   □ cm   1 m
                         100 cm
```

c
```
0   □   0.5   □   1 kg
```

d
```
0   □ g   500 g   □ g   1 kg
                        1000 g
```

e
```
0   □   0.5   □   1 litre
```

f
```
0   □ ml   500 ml   □ ml   1 litre
                           1000 ml
```

4 Copy and complete.

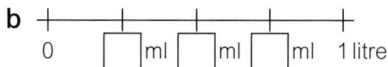

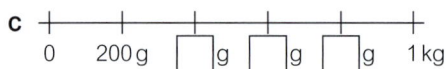

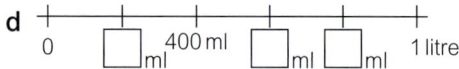

a
```
0   □ g   □ g   □ g   1 kg
```

b
```
0   □ ml   □ ml   □ ml   1 litre
```

c
```
0   200 g   □ g   □ g   □ g   1 kg
```

d
```
0   □ ml   400 ml   □ ml   □ ml   1 litre
```

5 Write the number shown by each arrow.

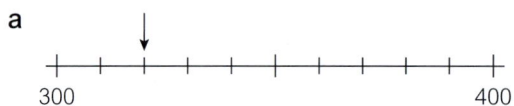

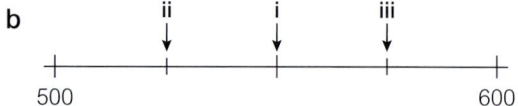

a
```
          ↓
300                         400
```

b
```
         ii        i        iii
         ↓         ↓        ↓
500                              600
```

Q5a hint Try counting up in different steps. What size step takes you to 400?

Reflect   Look at each of these scales. Discuss with a partner what is wrong with each scale.

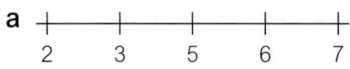

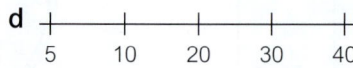

a
```
2   3   5   6   7
```

b
```
0   1       2   3
```

c
```
0 1 2 3 4   5   6
```

d
```
5   10   20   30   40
```

4.4 Working with decimals mentally

- Multiply decimals by multiples of 10, 100 and 1000
- Multiply decimals mentally
- Understand where to position the decimal point by considering equivalent calculations

Multiplying decimals

Guided

1 Copy and complete. Some parts have been done for you.

a $0.1 = 1 \div 10$ **b** $0.2 = 2 \div \square$ **c** $0.3 = 3 \div \square$ **d** $0.4 = \square \div \square$

e $0.01 = 1 \div 100$ **f** $0.02 = 2 \div \square$ **g** $0.03 = 3 \div \square$ **h** $0.04 = \square \div \square$

Guided

2 Copy and complete each calculation.

a 3×0.4	**b** 5×0.7	**c** 8×0.9	**d** 9×0.3
$= 3 \times 4 \div 10$	$= 5 \times 7 \div 10$	$= 8 \times 9 \div 10$	$= 9 \times 3 \div 10$
$= 12 \div 10$	$= 35 \div \square$	$= 72 \div \square$	$= \square \div \square$
$= \square$	$= \square$	$= \square$	$= \square$
e 3×0.04	**f** 5×0.07	**g** 8×0.09	**h** 9×0.03
$= 3 \times 4 \div 100$	$= 5 \times 7 \div 100$	$= 8 \times 9 \div \square$	$= 9 \times 3 \div \square$
$= 12 \div 100$	$= 35 \div \square$	$= 72 \div \square$	$= \square \div \square$
$= \square$	$= \square$	$= \square$	$= \square$

3 **Problem-solving** The answer to each of these questions is: 12, 1.2 or 0.12.

By thinking about how many times to divide or multiply by 10, write the correct answer to each question.

a 4×3 **b** 4×0.3 **c** 4×0.03 **d** 3×4

e 3×0.4 **f** 3×0.04

g 0.4×3 **h** 0.4×0.3

> **Q3g hint** 0.4×3 is the same as $4 \div 10 \times 3 = 4 \times 3 \div 10$

i 0.4×30 **j** 0.3×4

k 0.3×0.4 **l** 0.3×40

> **Q3i hint** 0.4×30 is the same as
> $4 \div 10 \times 3 \times 10 = 4 \times 3 \div 10 \times 10$

m 0.04×3 **n** 0.04×30

o 0.04×300 **p** 0.03×4 **q** 0.03×40 **r** 0.03×400

Using partitioning to multiply

1 Match a calculation in column A to an equivalent one in column B.

A	B
5×30	$7 \times 8 \times 100$
7×800	$4 \times 5 \times 10$
7×90	$5 \times 3 \times 10$
4×50	$8 \times 3 \times 100$
8×300	$7 \times 9 \times 10$

2 Use your answers to **Q1** to work out

    a 5×30 **b** 7×800 **c** 7×90

    d 4×50 **e** 8×300

Guided

3 Copy and complete. The first one has been done for you.

> **Q3 hint** $2 \times 10 = 10 \times 2$

    a $3.4 \times 20 = 3.4 \times 2 \times 10$

                  $= 3.4 \times 10 \times 2$

                  $= 34 \times 2$

                  $= \square$

    b $2.1 \times 30 = 2.1 \times 3 \times \square$

                  $= 2.1 \times \square \times 3$

                  $= \square \times 3$

                  $= \square$

    c $1.7 \times 50 = 1.7 \times 5 \times \square$

                  $= 1.7 \times \square \times 5$

                  $= \square \times 5$

                  $= \square$

Guided

4 Maria calculates 32×4 mentally like this.

> First I split 32 into tens and ones.

> Then I multiply each part by 4.

> Finally I add these two values together.

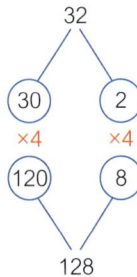

32

$30 \quad 2$

$\times 4 \quad \times 4$

$120 \quad 8$

128

Use Maria's method to work out

    a 53×5 **b** 53×0.5 **c** 71×3 **d** 71×0.3

    e 28×7 **f** 28×0.7 **g** 92×4 **h** 92×0.4

Using one calculation to work out another

1 **Problem-solving**

    a Work out 17×9.

    b Copy and complete, using your answer to part **a** to help find the answers.

        i $1.7 \times 9 = 17 \times 9 \div 10 = \square$ **ii** $17 \times 0.9 = 17 \times 9 \div \square = \square$

        iii $0.17 \times 9 = 17 \times 9 \div \square = \square$ **iv** $17 \times 0.09 = 17 \times 9 \div \square = \square$

2 **Reasoning**   Given that $32 \times 7 = 224$, without doing any calculations write down the answer to

    a 32×0.7 **b** 32×0.07

    c Explain how you worked out your answer to part **a**.

> **Reflect** $34 \times 0.1 = 34 \times 1 \div 10 = 34 \div 10 = 3.4$
>
> $1 \div 10 = 0.1$, so multiplying by 0.1 is equivalent to dividing by 10.
>
> What is multiplying by 0.01 equivalent to?

4.5 Working with decimals

- Add and subtract decimals
- Multiply and divide decimals

Adding and subtracting decimals

> **Worked example**
>
> Work out
>
> **a** 0.4 + 0.9
> 4 tenths + 9 tenths = 1 one and 3 tenths = 1.3
>
> **b** 1.6 − 0.7
> 1 one and 6 tenths − 7 tenths = 9 tenths = 0.9

1 Work out

    a 0.3 + 0.2 = ☐   **b** 0.1 + 2.2 = ☐   **c** 0.4 + 0.7 = ☐   **d** 4.3 + 0.6 = ☐

    e 0.9 − 0.1 = ☐   **f** 5.7 − 1.2 = ☐   **g** 1.2 − 0.4 = ☐   **h** 6.4 − 1.4 = ☐

2 Work out

    a 4.6 + 2.7   **b** 1.2 + 3.2

    c 5.6 + 4.9   **d** 3.1 + 4.7 + 1.2

    e 4.5 − 3.2   **f** 6.8 − 2.9

> **Q2a hint** Use a number line to help.
>
> +1   +1   +0.7
>
> 4   4.6 5 5.6 6 6.6 7 7.3   8

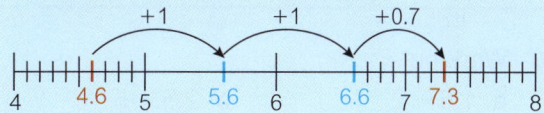

Decimal column addition and subtraction

> **Worked example**
>
> Use the column method to work out 75.9 + 56.3.
>
> ```
>  75.9
> +56.3
> ─────
> ```
> Line up the tens, ones and tenths.
>
> ```
>  75.9
> +56.3
> ─────
>     2
>    1
> ```
> Add the tenths. This gives 12, so write a small 1 in the ones coumn.
>
> ```
>  75.9
> +56.3
> ─────
> 132.2
>  1 1
> ```
> Bring down the decimal point and repeat for each column.

1 Use the column method to work out

    a 12.5 + 22.3   **b** 67.3 + 21.9   **c** 58.6 + 89.2   **d** 67.8 + 45.5

> **Worked example**
>
> Use the column method to work out 39.1 − 18.3.
>
> ```
>  39.1
> −18.3
> ─────
> ```
> Line up the tens, ones and tenths.
>
> ```
>     8
>  3⁹.¹1
> −18.3
> ─────
>     8
> ```
> Subtract the tenths. Take 1 from the ones to make 11 tenths.
>
> ```
>     8
>  3⁹.¹1
> −18.3
> ─────
> 20.8
> ```
> Bring down the decimal point and repeat for each column.

2 Use the column method to work out

    a 11.9 − 10.1   **b** 28.4 − 15.8   **c** 54.3 − 18.1   **d** 41.1 − 28.7

Multiplying decimals

Work out 3 × 4.1.

$$\begin{array}{r} 41 \\ \times\ \ 3 \\ \hline 123 \end{array}$$

Do the calculation ignoring the decimal point.

3 × 4.1 ≈ 3 × 4
3 × 4 = 12

Then estimate the answer.

4.1 × 3 = 12.3

Then add the decimal point into your answer.

1 Work out
    a 4.2 × 3   **b** 3.1 × 7   **c** 5.1 × 8   **d** 6.2 × 4

Q1 hint Estimate your answer to check if it's correct.

Dividing decimals

Worked example

Work out 1.2 ÷ 3.
1 whole and 2 tenths = 12 tenths
12 tenths ÷ 3 = 4 tenths
1.2 ÷ 3 = 0.4

1 unit 2 tenths

1.2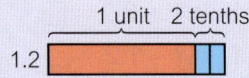

1 Work out
    a 1.6 ÷ 2   **b** 2.5 ÷ 5   **c** 5.4 ÷ 6   **d** 2.8 ÷ 4

Worked example

Work out 59.2 ÷ 4.

$$4\overline{)5^19.2}$$ 1☐.☐

How many 4s go into 5? 1 remainder 1. The remainder goes next to the 9.

$$4\overline{)5^19.^32}$$ 14.☐

How may 4s go into 19? 4 remainder 3. Repeat until the end.

$$4\overline{)5^19.^32}$$ 14.8

Once finished your answer is 14.8.

2 Work out
    a 85.5 ÷ 5   **b** 21.3 ÷ 3   **c** 50.4 ÷ 7   **d** 29.7 ÷ 9

Q2 hint Lay out like the worked example.

3 **Problem-solving** What is the change from £10 for each amount?
    a £3.50   **b** £8.40   **c** £5.85   **d** £9.89

Q3 hint You can write £10 as £10.00

4 **Problem-solving** Charles was selling books for £1.50 each. He made £54. How many books did he sell?

Reflect For each of these calculations decide whether **i**, **ii** or **iii** is correct. Discuss with a partner how you got your answer.
a 1.2 × 9   **i** 1.08   **ii** 10.8   **iii** 1.8
b 9.6 ÷ 6   **i** 1.6   **ii** 1.06   **iii** 0.16

4.6 Perimeter

- Work out the perimeter of squares, rectangles and regular polygons
- Calculate the perimeter of shapes made from rectangles

Perimeter of squares and rectangles

Key point The perimeter is the total distance around the edge of a shape.
Add the lengths of all the sides to work out the perimeter of a shape.

1 **Reasoning** These rectangles are drawn on centimetre squared paper.

   a Find the perimeter by counting squares all the way around each shape.

   b Write the length of each side. What do you notice about opposite sides?

   c Add the lengths together to find the perimeter of each rectangle. Is it the same as in part **a**?

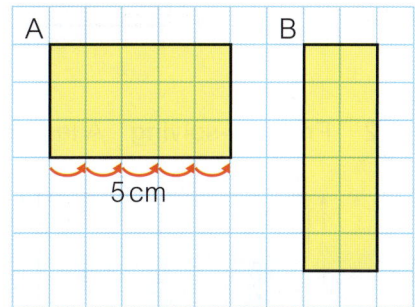

2 a What are the lengths of the unmarked sides of this square?

   b Work out the perimeter.

3 a What are the lengths of the unmarked sides of this rectangle?

   b Work out the perimeter.

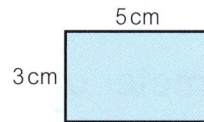

4 These shapes are drawn on centimetre squared paper. Work out the perimeter of each shape.

Q4 hint Each grid length is 1 cm.

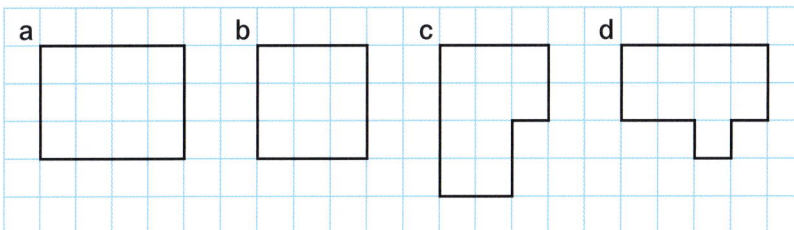

5 A square tile has sides of length 4 cm. What is its perimeter?

Q5 hint Sketch and label the tile.

6 The base of a rectangular box has length 26 cm and width 38 cm. What is its perimeter?

Q6 hint Sketch and label the rectangle.

7 A square room has sides of length 4.7 m. Work out the perimeter of the room.

8 A baking tray has width 46.5 cm and length 33.2 cm. Work out the perimeter.

Perimeter of shapes made from rectangles

1   This shape is made by joining two rectangles together.
    a   What are the lengths of A and B?
    b   Work out the perimeter.

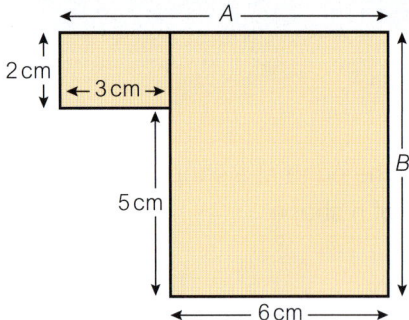

Q1 hint Look at the sides parallel to A and then add them together. Do the same for B.

2   **Problem-solving**   A fence is going to be built around the perimeter of this garden.

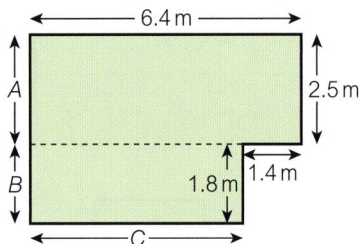

    a   Work out the lengths A, B and C.
    b   Work out the total length of fence needed.

Q2a hint C = ☐ – ☐

Perimeter of polygons

> **Key point**   A polygon with **all sides** the same length and angles the same size is a **regular polygon**.

1   a   Write the other side lengths of this regular pentagon and regular hexagon.
    b   Work out the perimeter of each polygon.

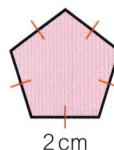

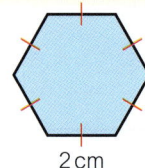

2   Work out the perimeter of
    a   a regular hexagon with sides of length 6 cm
    b   a regular pentagon with sides of length 5 cm
    c   a regular octagon with sides of length 3 cm
    d   a regular nonagon with sides of length 4 cm

> **Reflect**   Discuss with a partner a method for finding the perimeter of
> a   a rectangle   b   a square   c   a regular pentagon
> d   a regular hexagon   e   any regular polygon

4.7 Area

- Find areas of shapes by counting squares
- Find the area of rectangles and squares
- Calculate the area of shapes made from rectangles

Finding area by counting squares

> **Key point** Area is the space inside a shape.
> Area is measured using square units.
> 1 cm $\square$ one square centimetre = 1 cm^2

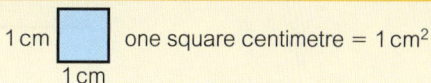

1 These shapes are drawn on centimetre squared paper.

   a Find the area of each shape by counting the number of squares inside.

   b Multiply the length by the width of each shape to find the area. Is it the same as in part **a**?

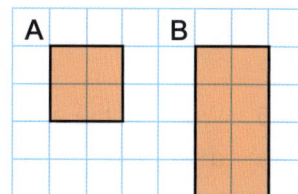

2 In cm^2, calculate the area of each shape by counting the squares.

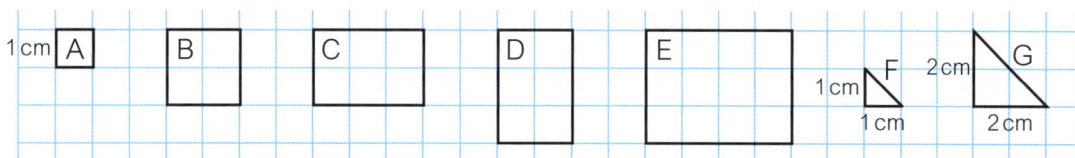

Area of rectangles and squares

> **Key point** Area of a rectangle = length × width
> width
> ← length →

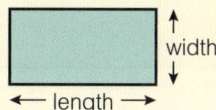

Guided

1 Copy and complete.

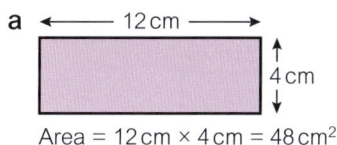

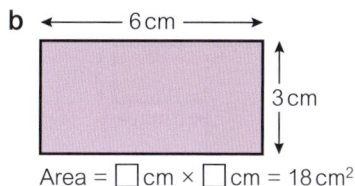

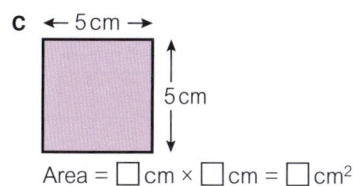

   a ← 12 cm →
   4 cm
   Area = 12 cm × 4 cm = 48 cm^2

   b ← 6 cm →
   3 cm
   Area = $\square$ cm × $\square$ cm = 18 cm^2

   c ← 5 cm →
   5 cm
   Area = $\square$ cm × $\square$ cm = $\square$ cm^2

2 Work out the area of each rectangle.

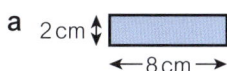

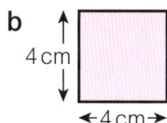

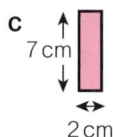

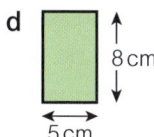

   a 2 cm $\updownarrow$ ← 8 cm →

   b 4 cm ← 4 cm →

   c 7 cm 2 cm

   d 8 cm 5 cm

   Q2 hint
   Area = $\square$ × $\square$ = $\square$ cm^2

3 Find the area of each rectangle.

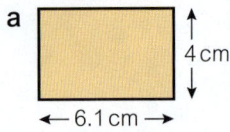

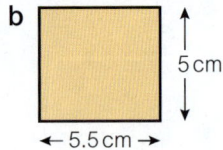

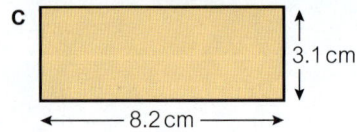

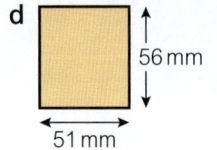

Q3d hint Area = ☐ × ☐ = ☐mm²

a
4 cm
←6.1 cm→

b
5 cm
← 5.5 cm →

c
3.1 cm
←———— 8.2 cm ————→

d
56 mm
←——51 mm——→

4 **a** Work out the area of each square.

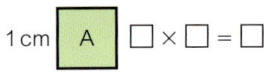

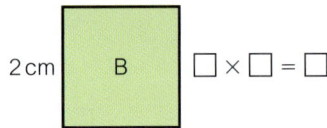

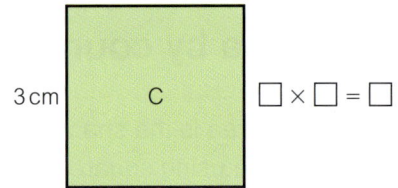

1 cm | A | ☐ × ☐ = ☐

2 cm | B | ☐ × ☐ = ☐

3 cm | C | ☐ × ☐ = ☐

b Work out the area of the next square in the pattern.

c **Reasoning** Look at the areas you have calculated. What kind of numbers are they?

5 Work out the area of a square with side length

a 9 cm   **b** 25 mm   **c** 0.7 cm   **d** 2.4 mm

6 **Problem-solving** Draw a rectangle on squared paper with an area of

a 10 cm²   **b** 14 cm²   **c** 5 cm²

Q7a hint Think of two numbers that multiply to give 10.

Area of shapes made from rectangles

Guided

1 Copy and complete the workings to find the total area of this shape.

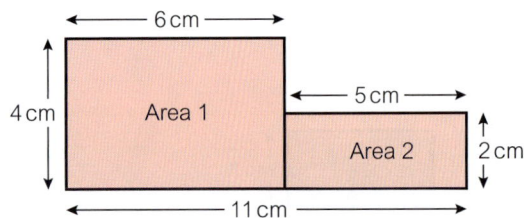

←—— 6 cm ——→
4 cm | Area 1
←— 5 cm —→
Area 2 | 2 cm
←———— 11 cm ————→

Area 1 = length × width
= 6 cm × 4 cm = ☐ cm²
Area 2 = length × width
= ☐ cm × ☐ cm = ☐ cm²
Total Area = Area 1 + Area 2
= ☐ cm² + ☐ cm²
= ☐ cm²

2 These shapes are made by putting two rectangles together. Work out the area of each shape.

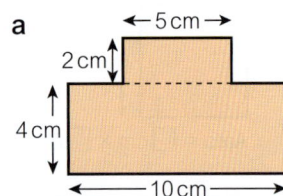

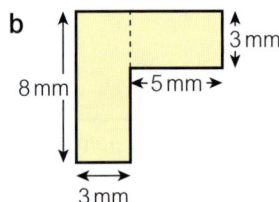

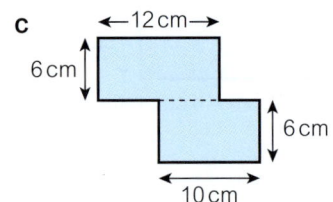

a
←5 cm→
2 cm
4 cm
←——10 cm——→

b
8 mm
3 mm
←5 mm→
←→ 3 mm

c
←12 cm→
6 cm
6 cm
←——10 cm——→

Reflect What information do you need to work out the area of these shapes?

a rectangle   **b** square

4.8 More units of measure

- Choose suitable units to measure area
- Use units of measure to solve problems
- Use metric and imperial units

Choosing suitable units of measure

1 Choose the most suitable units for each measure.
   Select your answer from this list.

m	km	g	litres	mm	ml	kg

   a length   **b** capacity   **c** mass

2 Put these units of measure in order from smallest to largest.
   a mm   km   cm   m   **b** cm^2 km^2 mm^2 m^2

3 **Problem-solving**   From the units in **Q2**, choose the most suitable unit of area to measure
   a the area of France   **b** the area of a TV screen   **c** the area of a football pitch
   d the area of a 5p coin   **e** the area of a phone screen

Converting metric units

> **Key point**   Some more metric units that you need to know are
> Mass: 1 tonne (t) = 1000 kg   Area: 1 hectare (ha) = $10000 m^2$
>
> $\times 1000$: t ⇄ kg : $\div 1000$ $\times 10000$: ha ⇄ m : $\div 10000$

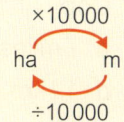

1 Copy and complete.
   a $3t = 3 \times 1000 = \square\,kg$ **b** $4t = 4 \times \square = \square\,kg$ **c** $7000\,kg = 7000 \div 1000 = \square\,t$
   d $5000\,kg = 5000 \div \square = \square\,t$ **e** $9t = \square \times \square = \square\,kg$ **f** $12000\,kg = \square \div \square = \square\,t$

2 Copy and complete.
   a $5\,ha = 5 \times 10000 = \square\,m^2$ **b** $80000\,m^2 = 80000 \div 10000 = \square\,ha$
   c $7\,ha = 7 \times \square = \square\,m^2$ **d** $40000\,m^2 = 40000 \div \square = \square\,ha$
   e $15\,ha = \square \times \square = \square\,m^2$ **f** $220000\,m^2 = \square \div \square = \square\,ha$

> **Key point**   Capacity: 1 litre = 1000 ml
>
> $\times 1000$: litres ⇄ ml : $\div 1000$

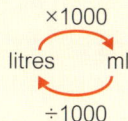

3 Copy and complete. The first one has been done for you.   **Q3 hint** 1 ml = $1\,cm^3$
   a $4\,ml = 4\,cm^3$ **b** $6\,cm^3 = \square\,ml$
   c $12\,ml = \square\,cm^3$ **d** $22\,cm^3 = \square\,ml$

4 Copy and complete.

Q4 hint Remember that 1 litre = 1000 ml

   a 5 litres = 5 × 1000 = 5000 ml = ☐ cm³
   b 7 litres = 7 × ☐ = ☐ ml = ☐ cm³
   c 12 000 cm³ = 12 000 ml = 12 000 ÷ 1000 = ☐ litres
   d 8000 cm³ = ☐ ml = ☐ ÷ ☐ = ☐ litres

5 **Problem-solving**   The average farm in the UK is 57 ha, and the average field is 12 ha.
   a Work out how many m² the average farm is.
   b Work out how many m² the average field is.
   c Work out how many fields with an area of 12 ha each would fit into an area of 600 000 m²

Converting metric and imperial measures

> **Key point**   You need to know these length conversions between metric and imperial units.
>
> 1 foot (ft) ≈ 30 cm   1 mile ≈ 1.6 km   ≈ means approximately
>
>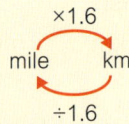

1 Copy and complete these approximations.
   a 2 ft ≈ 2 × 30 = ☐ cm   **b** 30 cm ≈ ☐ ft   **c** 120 cm ≈ 120 ÷ 30 = ☐ ft
   d 12 ft ≈ 12 × ☐ = ☐ cm   **e** 8 ft ≈ ☐ × ☐ = ☐ cm   **f** 360 cm ≈ ☐ ÷ ☐ = ☐ ft

2 Copy and complete these approximations.
   a 7 miles ≈ 7 × 1.6 = ☐ km   **b** 8 km ≈ 8 ÷ 1.6 = ☐ miles   **c** 14 miles ≈ 14 × ☐ = ☐ km
   d 12 km ≈ 12 ÷ ☐ = ☐ miles   **e** 22 miles ≈ ☐ × ☐ = ☐ km   **f** 24 km ≈ ☐ ÷ ☐ = ☐ miles

3 **Problem-solving**   Dani is 5 ft tall. Approximately how tall is she in cm?

4 **Problem-solving**   A car holds 40 litres of fuel. Write what this is in
   a millilitres   **b** cm³

5 **Problem-solving**   An African bush elephant weighs 6 t and an Asian elephant weighs 5.4 t.
   a How much does the African bush elephant weigh in kg?
   b How much does the Asian elephant weigh in kg?
   c Work out the difference between the weight of the
   African bush elephant and the Asian elephant in
      i tonnes   **ii** kilograms

Q6c hint

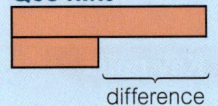

difference

> **Reflect**   Write a list of the units of measure you have come across and group them.
> Discuss with a partner
> **a** which of the units are new to you and which you knew before
> **b** how you grouped your units and why

5 Fractions and percentages

5.1 Comparing fractions

- Use fraction notation to describe parts of a shape
- Compare simple fractions

Using fractions to describe parts of shapes

1 Copy and continue this sequence of fraction diagrams.

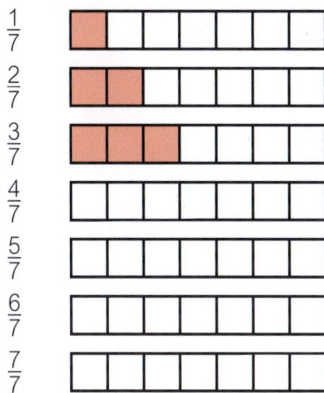

$\frac{1}{7}$

$\frac{2}{7}$

$\frac{3}{7}$

$\frac{4}{7}$

$\frac{5}{7}$

$\frac{6}{7}$

$\frac{7}{7}$

Key point

$\frac{2}{7}$ → number of shaded parts
→ total number of parts

2 Match the pairs of bars that have the same fraction shaded. Write the pairs of letters.

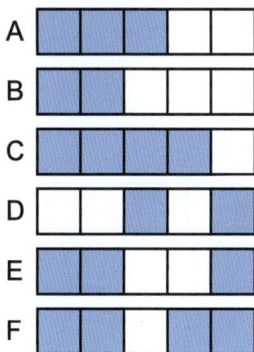

A

B

C

D

E

F

3 What fraction of each shape is shaded?

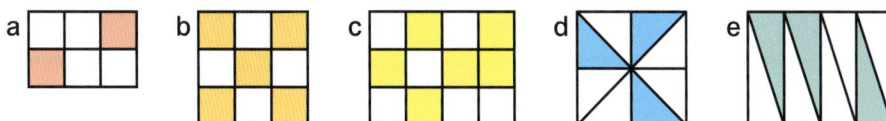

a   b   c   d   e

Ordering fractions

1   **a** What fraction of each bar is shaded?

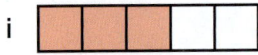

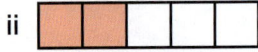

     i

     ii

     iii

    b Write your answers to part **a** in order from smallest to largest.

2   **Problem-solving**   Angie eats $\frac{2}{5}$ of a pizza. Ian eats $\frac{1}{5}$. Who eats more?

3   **a** Draw three bars the same length, like this:

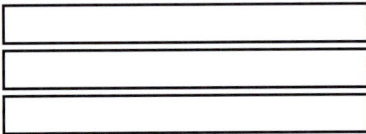

    b Shade them to show $\frac{1}{4}$, $\frac{3}{4}$ and $\frac{2}{4}$.

    c Write $\frac{1}{4}$, $\frac{3}{4}$, $\frac{2}{4}$ in ascending order (from smallest to largest).

4   Write each set of fractions in ascending order.

    a $\frac{7}{8}$ $\frac{1}{8}$ $\frac{3}{8}$
             b $\frac{3}{10}$ $\frac{9}{10}$ $\frac{7}{10}$

    c $\frac{7}{12}$ $\frac{5}{12}$ $\frac{1}{12}$ $\frac{11}{12}$
        d $\frac{5}{13}$ $\frac{7}{13}$ $\frac{11}{13}$ $\frac{2}{13}$ $\frac{4}{13}$

5   **a** What fraction of each bar is shaded?

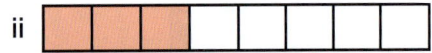

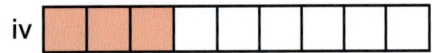

     i   **ii**

     iii   **iv**

    b Order the fractions in part **a** from smallest to largest.

> **Reflect**   Two fractions have different denominators. Both have numerator 1. How can you decide which is larger?

5.2 Simplifying fractions

- Change an improper fraction to a mixed number
- Identify equivalent fractions
- Simplify fractions by dividing the numerator and denominator by common factors

Changing improper fractions to mixed numbers

Key point
$\frac{4}{3}$ is an **improper fraction** because its numerator is larger than its denominator.
$1\frac{1}{3}$ is a **mixed number** because it has a whole number part (1) and a fraction part $\left(\frac{1}{3}\right)$.

1 a **Problem-solving** Ami cuts a pie into halves. How many pieces are there?
  b Work out how many pieces there will be if she cuts a pie into
    i thirds ii quarters iii fifths

Worked example

Write $\frac{5}{3}$ as a mixed number.

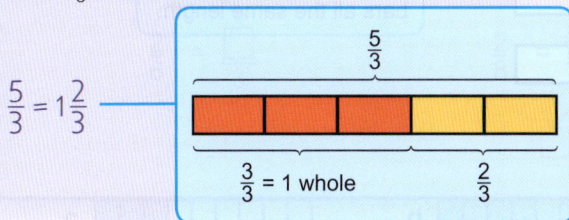

$\frac{5}{3} = 1\frac{2}{3}$

$$\frac{5}{3}$$

$\frac{3}{3}$ = 1 whole $\frac{2}{3}$

2 Write these improper fractions as mixed numbers.

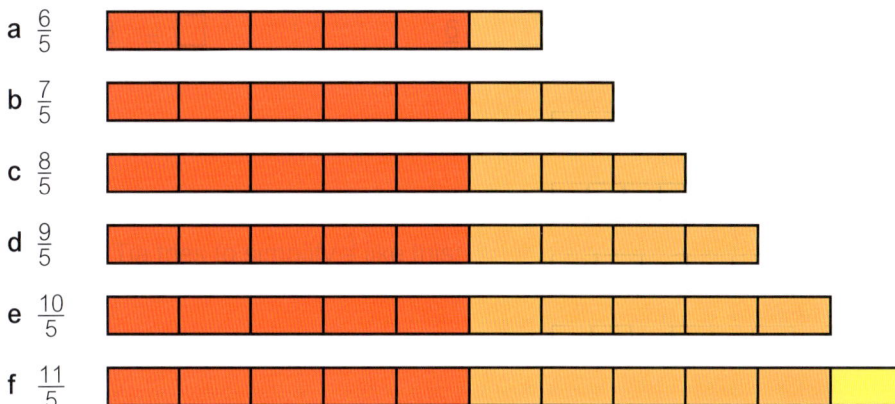

a $\frac{6}{5}$

b $\frac{7}{5}$

c $\frac{8}{5}$

d $\frac{9}{5}$

e $\frac{10}{5}$

f $\frac{11}{5}$

3 Write these improper fractions as mixed numbers.

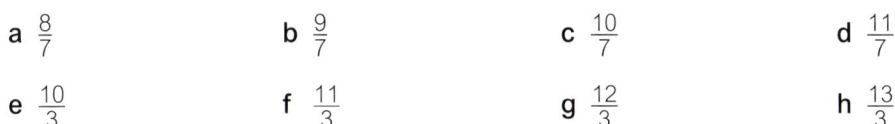

a $\frac{8}{7}$ b $\frac{9}{7}$ c $\frac{10}{7}$ d $\frac{11}{7}$

e $\frac{10}{3}$ f $\frac{11}{3}$ g $\frac{12}{3}$ h $\frac{13}{3}$

5.5 Understanding percentages

- Understand percentages as 'the number of parts per 100'
- Convert a percentage to a fraction or decimal

Understanding percentages

Worked example

What percentage of this grid is shaded?

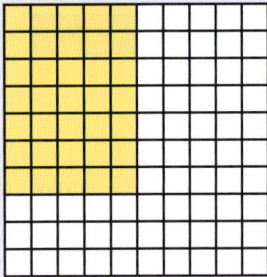

There are 100 squares. 35 out of the 100 squares are shaded.

35% is shaded.

1 What percentage of each grid is shaded?

a
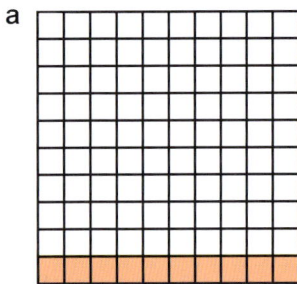

b
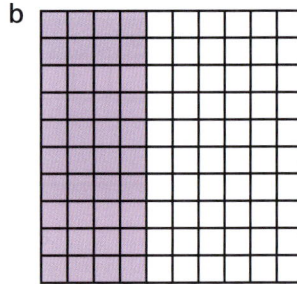

c
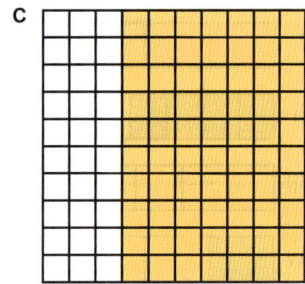

d
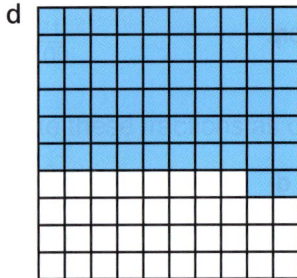

e
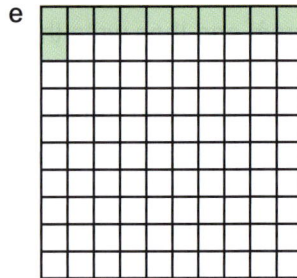

f
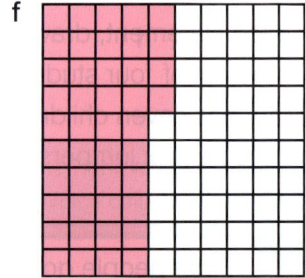

g
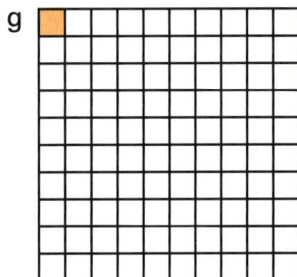

h
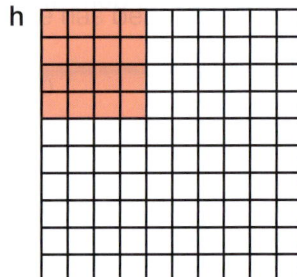

i
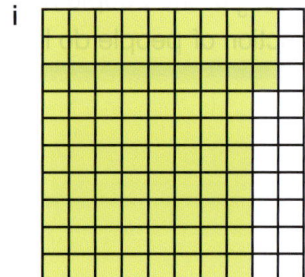

Converting percentages to fractions and decimals

Worked example

Write 17% as

a a fraction

$17\% = \dfrac{17}{100}$ —— 17% means '17 out of 100'.

b a decimal

$17\% = \dfrac{17}{100} = 0.17$ —— Write 17% as a fraction. Then use place value knowledge to convert the fraction to a decimal.

Guided

1 Copy and complete to write each percentage as a fraction, then as a decimal.

a $91\% = \dfrac{\square}{100} = 0.91$ **b** $23\% = \dfrac{\square}{100} = 0.\square\square$ **c** $37\% = \dfrac{\square}{\square} = 0.\square\square$

d $33\% = \dfrac{\square}{\square} = \square.\square\square$ **e** $71\% = \dfrac{\square}{\square} = \square.\square\square$ **f** $97\% = \dfrac{\square}{\square} = \square.\square\square$

2 Write these percentages as decimals.

   a 34%   **b** 92%   **c** 18%

   d 45%   **e** 95%

Guided

3 Write these percentages as fractions in their simplest form.
The first one has been done for you.

a $50\% = \dfrac{50}{100} = \dfrac{1}{2}$ **b** $25\% = \dfrac{\square}{100} = \dfrac{\square}{4}$ **c** $30\% = \dfrac{\square}{100} = \dfrac{\square}{10}$

d $45\% = \dfrac{\square}{100} = \dfrac{\square}{20}$ **e** $40\% = \dfrac{\square}{100} = \dfrac{\square}{5}$ **f** $14\% = \dfrac{\square}{100} = \dfrac{\square}{\square}$

Converting decimals to percentages

Guided

1 Write each decimal as a fraction with denominator 100, and then as a percentage.

a $0.54 = \dfrac{\square}{100} = \square\%$ **b** $0.28 = \dfrac{\square}{100} = \square\%$ **c** $0.07 = \dfrac{\square}{100} = \square\%$

Guided

2 Write each decimal as a fraction with denominator 100, and then as a percentage.

a $0.1 = \dfrac{\square}{10} = \dfrac{\square}{100} = \square\%$ **b** $0.3 = \dfrac{\square}{10} = \dfrac{\square}{100} = \square\%$ **c** $0.9 = \dfrac{\square}{10} = \dfrac{\square}{100} = \square\%$

Reflect

Jamal writes: $30\% = \dfrac{30}{100} = \dfrac{6}{20}$

Explain why he hasn't written the percentage as a fraction in its simplest form.
What does he need to do to write it in its simplest form?

5.6 Percentages of amounts

- Calculate percentages

Calculating 50%, 25% and 75%

> **Key point**
>
> $50\% = \frac{1}{2}$
> To find 50% of an amount, divide by 2.
> $25\% = \frac{1}{4}$
> To find 25% of an amount, divide by 4.
>
>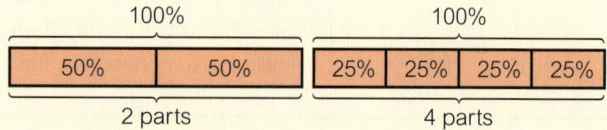

Guided

1 Work out

    a 50% of 30 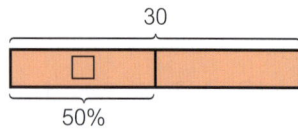 $30 \div 2 =$

    b 50% of 300 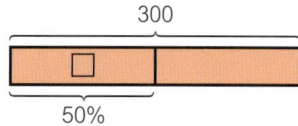 $300 \div 2 =$

    c 50% of 12 = ☐ ÷ ☐ =   **d** 50% of 120 = ☐ ÷ ☐ =

Guided

2 Work out

    a 25% of £20 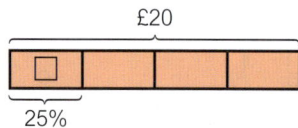 $£20 \div 4 =$

    b 25% of 60p   **c** 25% of 16 miles   **d** 25% of 24 cm

Guided

3 **Reasoning** Work out

    a 75% of £40 = 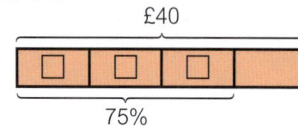 $3 \times £☐ = £☐$

    b 75% of 32 kg =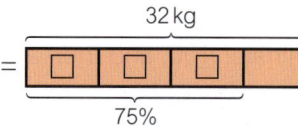

    c 75% of 16 miles   **d** 75% of 24 cm   **e** 75% of 2000 kg   **f** 75% of 80 litres

Calculating 10%, 20%, 30%, ...

> **Key point**
>
> $10\% = \frac{1}{10}$
> To find 10% of an amount, divide by 10.
>
>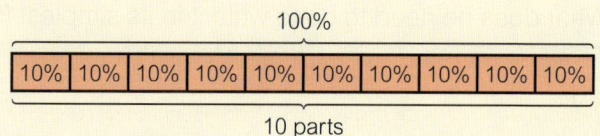

Guided

1 Work out

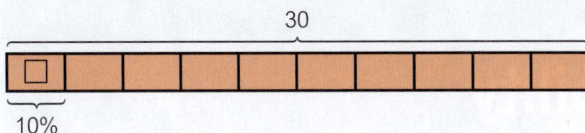

a 10% of 30

b 10% of 300

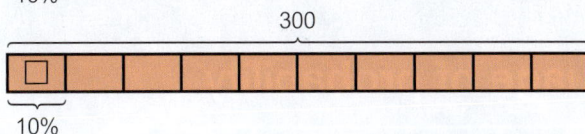

c 10% of 120 = ☐ ÷ ☐ =   **d** 10% of 1200 = ☐ ÷ ☐ =

e 10% of 3600 =   **f** 10% of 360 =

2 Find 10% of

a 70 cm   **b** £400   **c** 190 g

d 20 miles   **e** 50p   **f** 330 ml

Guided

3 Work out

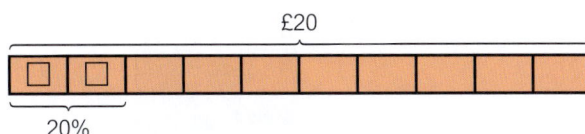

a 20% of £20   2 × £☐ =

b 30% of £20   **c** 40% of £20   **d** 70% of £20   **e** 90% of £20

4 Work out

a 10% of 500   **b** 30% of 500   **c** 50% of 500   **d** 80% of 500   **e** 100% of 500

Calculating 1%

> **Key point**
>
> $1\% = \frac{1}{100}$
>
> To find 1% of an amount, divide by 100.
>
> 100%
>
> 100 parts

Guided

1 Copy and complete.

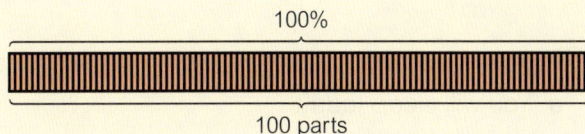

a 1% of 200   200 ÷ 100 =

1% = ☐

b 1% of 2000 = 2000 ÷ 100 =

c 1% of 400 = ☐ ÷ ☐ =   **d** 1% of 4000 = ☐ ÷ ☐ =

e 1% of 2300 = ☐ ÷ ☐ =   **f** 1% of 3300 = ☐ ÷ ☐ =

2 Find 1% of

a 400 cm   **b** 1200 g   **d** 1900 mm

e 3000 miles   **f** 700p   **g** £20 000

> **Reflect**   Jessica says: 'To find 50% you need to find 10% and then multiply your answer by 5.' Is Jessica correct? How else could she calculate 50%? Which method would **you** use?

6 Probability

6.1 The language of probability

- Use the language of probability
- Use a probability scale with words
- Understand the probability scale from 0 to 1

Probability in words

1 Match each description to a probability.

An event	The probability is
A can't happen	**1** unlikely
B often happens	**2** likely
C rarely happens	**3** certain
D happens and doesn't happen equally often	**4** impossible
E always happens	**5** even chance

2 Put these probability statements in order, from least likely to most likely.

unlikely   impossible   certain   even chance   likely

3 **Problem-solving** Describe the probability of each event using the words from **Q2**.
   a You will sleep today.
   b You will go to the moon.
   c If you flip a coin it will land tails up.
   d The month after April will be May.
   e You can run a mile in 1 second.

4 **Problem-solving** Put each of the probability statements from **Q2** on this probability scale.

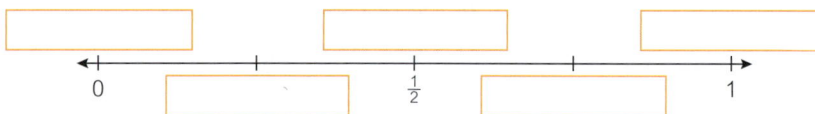

5 Draw three copies of this spinner.
Shade each spinner in turn so that the probability
of landing on a shaded segment is
   a even chance   **b** unlikely   **c** certain

Probability scale from 0 to 1

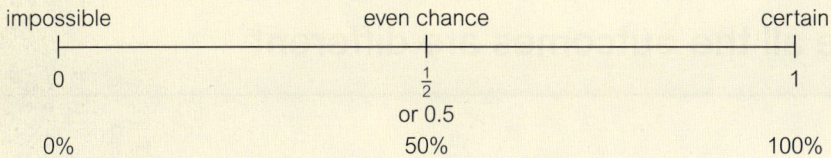

impossible	even chance	certain
0	$\frac{1}{2}$ or 0.5	1
0%	50%	100%

1 What are the missing values on these scales?

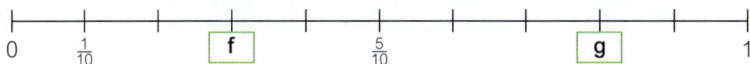

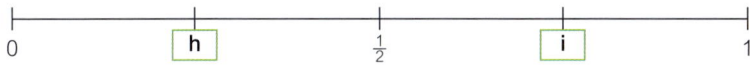

0 0.1 **a** 0.3 0.4 0.5 **b** 0.7 0.8 0.9 1

0 10% **c** 30% **d** 50% 60% 70% 80% **e** 100%

0 $\frac{1}{10}$ **f** $\frac{5}{10}$ **g** 1

0 **h** $\frac{1}{2}$ **i** 1

Guided

2 Problem-solving   Copy this probability scale.

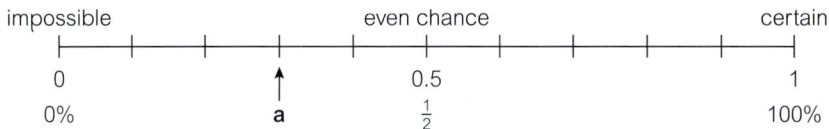

impossible	even chance	certain
0	0.5	1
0%	**a**	$\frac{1}{2}$	100%

Mark the probability of each event on your probability scale. The first one has been done for you.

a The probability of rain today is 30%.
b The probability that a newborn baby will be a girl is 50%.
c The probability that a person is left-handed is 0.1.
d The probability that a train is on time is $\frac{9}{10}$.

3 a Reasoning   What is the lowest number value a probability can have?
   b Reasoning   What is the highest number value a probability can have?

Reflect   In this lesson you have met some new words and learned about probability
scales. Write down what you think it means for an event to be
a impossible   **b** certain   **c** likely

6.2 Calculating probability

- Identify outcomes of an event
- Calculate probabilities

Probability where all the outcomes are different

Worked example

A ball is taken from this bag.

a List the possible outcomes. ——— 'Outcomes' are events that could occur.

Green, yellow, blue

b Write the total number of possible outcomes.

3

c How many successful outcomes are there for the event 'pick a blue ball'?

1

d Find the probability of picking a blue ball.

Probability of picking a blue ball = $\frac{1}{3}$

Number of successful outcomes

Total number of outcomes.

1 A ball is taken from this bag.
   a List the possible outcomes.
   b Write the total number of possible outcomes.
   c How many successful outcomes are there for the event 'pick a white ball'?
   d Find the probability of picking a white ball.

2 A fair six-sided dice is rolled.
   a List the possible outcomes.
   b Find the probability of rolling a 5.

3 A letter is picked at random from this set of cards
   a List the possible outcomes.
   b Find the probability of selecting 'M'.

M	A	T	H	S

4 A fair coin is flipped. What is the probability that it lands tails up?

Probability where some outcomes are the same

Key point There might be some outcomes that are the same.
For example, if you pick a letter from the word SEE, two of the outcomes are E and one is S.

1 A ball is taken from this bag.

List the 8 possible outcomes in the form 'W, W, W...'

2 A letter is selected at random from the word HELLO.

List the possible outcomes.

3 A card is selected at random from this set.

List the possible outcomes.

Worked example

A card is picked at random from this set.

Find the probability of picking a 2.

5 possible outcomes: 1, 2, 2, 2, 3

Probability of a 2 = $\frac{3}{5}$

Number of successful outcomes

Total number of outcomes.

4 A ball is picked at random from this bag.

a List the 3 possible outcomes.

b Find the probability of picking a blue ball.

5 A letter tile is selected at random from these tiles.

a List the possible outcomes.

b Find the probability of selecting an 'A'.

A A O R A

6 A letter is selected at random from the word EVENT.

Find the probability of selecting:

a V   **b** E

7 Find the probability of the spinner landing on green.

Reflect   Look at the spinner in **Q7**.

Which of these statements are true?

A The probability of landing on orange is $\frac{1}{2}$

B The probability of landing on yellow is $\frac{1}{3}$

C The probability of landing on yellow is $\frac{1}{6}$

6.3 More probability calculations

- Use probability notation
- Calculate the probability of an event *not* happening

Probability notation

Key point   P(X) means the probability of X happening.

Worked example

A card is selected at random from this set.   A B C
Work out P(A).

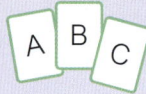

> P(A) means the probability of choosing A.

$$P(A) = \frac{1}{3}$$

> Number of cards showing A.

> Total number of cards.

1   A ball is selected at random from this bag.
Calculate

    a   P(red)   **b**   P(black)   **c**   P(blue)

2   Matt chooses a letter from the word BLACK.
Calculate

    a   P(B)   **b**   P(C)   **c**   P(K)

3   Pia spins this fair spinner once. Work out

    a   P(2)   **b**   P(4)   **c**   P(5)

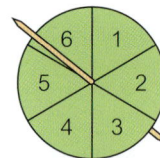

Probability of A or B

Worked example

A card is selected at random from this set.   A B C
Work out P(A or B).

> P(A or B) means the probability of choosing A or B.

$$P(A \text{ or } B) = \frac{2}{3}$$

> Number of cards showing A or B.

> Total number of cards.

1 Emily chooses a letter from the word

| S | P | I | N | N | E | R |

Work out

a P(S)   b P(N)   c P(S or N)

2 A fair six-sided dice is rolled.

Calculate

a P(5)   b P(1)   c P(1 or 5)

3 A card is selected at random from this set. Work out
a P(1)   b P(2)   c P(1 or 2)

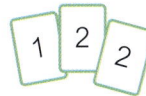

Probability of an event not happening

Key point   The sum of the probabilities of all possible outcomes of an event is 1.
If the two possible outcomes are P(1) and P(2), P(1) + P(2) = 1

1 a Work out the probability that this spinner will land on green or yellow.

b **Reasoning**   Natalia says: 'P(green or yellow) is the same as P(not blue).'
Is Natalia correct? Explain.

2 For the spinner in **Q1** write
a P(blue) as a percentage
b P(yellow or green or blue) as a percentage
c P(not blue) as a percentage

3 **Problem-solving**   A card is chosen at random from this set.
a Work out

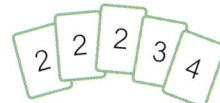

i P(2)   ii P(not 2)   iii P(3 or 4)
b Which two answers to part **a** are equal? Explain why.

Reflect   The probability of winning a game is 20%. Ami says if she knows the probability of winning, she also knows the probability of losing. How can she work this out?

6.4 Experimental probability

- Estimate probability based on experimental data

Experimental probability as a fraction

1   In a group of 16 students, 4 are left-handed.
    What fraction are left-handed? Simplify the fraction.

2   A frequency table shows the colour of cars in a showroom.
    a How many blue cars are in the showroom?
    b Work out the total frequency (total number of cars).
    c What fraction of the cars are blue?

Colour	Frequency
red	2
blue	7
grey	11
Total frequency	

> **Key point**   The results of an experiment can be used to calculate **experimental probability**.
> Experimental probability = $\dfrac{\text{frequency of event}}{\text{total frequency}}$

Worked example

Bella spins the spinner 25 times. She records the results in a table.
Calculate the experimental probability of landing on each colour.

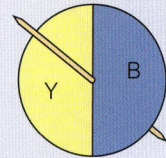

Colour	Frequency	Experimental probability
yellow	13	$\dfrac{13}{25}$ — $\dfrac{\text{frequency of yellow}}{\text{total frequency}}$
blue	12	$\dfrac{12}{25}$ — $\dfrac{\text{frequency of blue}}{\text{total frequency}}$
Total frequency	25	

3   Kyra records the eye colour of her friends.
    a Work out the total frequency.
    b Work out the experimental probability for blue.
    c Work out the experimental probability for brown.
    d Work out the experimental probability for green.

Eye colour	Frequency	Experimental probability
blue	2	
brown	4	
green	1	
Total frequency		

4   Henry has a trick coin. He flips it 20 times.
    It lands on heads 19 times.
    Copy and complete.

    a The experimental probability of landing on heads = $\dfrac{\square}{20}$

    b The experimental probability of landing on tails = $\dfrac{\square}{20}$

Experimental probability as a percentage

1 a $\frac{17}{100} = \square\%$ b $\frac{12}{50} = \frac{\square}{100} = \square\%$ c $\frac{7}{25} = \frac{\square}{100} = \square\%$

d $\frac{11}{20} = \frac{\square}{100} = \square\%$ e $\frac{3}{10} = \frac{\square}{100} = \square\%$ f $\frac{11}{50} = \frac{\square}{\square} = \square\%$

2 Mara records how some of her friends travel to school.

a What fraction of people walk to school?

b What fraction of people travel to school by bus?

c What fraction of people travel to school by car?

d What percentage of people walk to school?

e What percentage of people travel to school by bus?

f What percentage of people travel to school by car?

Method of Transport	Frequency
walk	3
bus	2
car	5
Total frequency	

3 This spinner is spun and the colour it lands on is recorded.

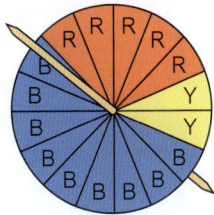

Colour	Frequency	Experimental probability
red	34	$\frac{\square}{100} = \square\%$
yellow	6	$\frac{\square}{100} = \square\%$
blue	60	$\frac{\square}{100} = \square\%$
Total frequency		

a Work out the total frequency.

b For each colour, work out the experimental probability as a fraction.
Then convert it to a percentage.

4 Raul and Charlie play noughts and crosses. The results are shown in the table.

Winner	Frequency	Experimental probability
Raul	11	$\frac{\square}{20} = \frac{\square}{100} = \square\%$
Charlie	9	$\frac{\square}{20} = \frac{\square}{100} = \square\%$
Total frequency:	20	

Work out these experimental probabilities as percentages:

a Raul wins   b Charlie wins

Reflect   If you flip a fair coin, the mathematical probability of it landing on heads is $\frac{1}{2}$.
If you do an experiment flipping a coin, is it certain to land on heads exactly $\frac{1}{2}$ of the time?

6.5 Expected outcomes

- Use probability to estimate the expected number of times an outcome will occur
- Apply probabilities from simple experimental data in simple situations

Calculating probability

1 There are 3 red balls and 1 white ball in a bag.

Erin says: 'Since there are two colours, the probability of choosing each colour is $\frac{1}{2}$.'

a Reasoning Explain why Erin is wrong.

b Give the probability of picking

  i a white ball   **ii** a red ball

2 A fair dice labelled 1, 2, 3, 4, 5 and 6 is rolled.

Work out

a P(2)   **b** P(even number)

c P(odd number)   **d** P(prime number)

e P(square number)

3 Arun rolls 1 on a fair dice.
What is the probability of him rolling a 1 on his next roll?

Expected outcomes

1 Copy and complete:

a $\frac{1}{2}$ of 120 = 120 ÷ 2 = ☐

  120
  | ? | |

b $\frac{1}{3}$ of 120 = 120 ÷ 3 = ☐

  120
  | ? | |

c $\frac{1}{4}$ × 120 = 120 ÷ 4 = ☐

d $\frac{1}{5}$ × 120 = ☐ ÷ ☐ = ☐

e $\frac{1}{6}$ × 120 = ☐ ÷ ☐ = ☐

f $\frac{1}{10}$ × 120 = ☐ ÷ ☐ = ☐

2 Work out

a $\frac{1}{3} \times 90$

90

| ? | | |

b $\frac{2}{3} \times 90$

90

| ? | ? | |

c $\frac{1}{4} \times 200$

d $\frac{3}{4} \times 90$

3 Rose knows that on a fair dice $P(2) = \frac{1}{6}$
Work out how many 2s she can expect to roll if she rolls a fair dice

> **Q3 hint** The expected outcome is that $\frac{1}{6}$ of the rolls will be 2s.

a 6 times   **b** 12 times   **c** 60 times   **d** 600 times

4 The probability of a set of traffic lights being red is $\frac{1}{3}$.
Work out how many times you can expect the traffic lights to be red if you drive through them

a 3 times   **b** 9 times   **c** 12 times   **d** 30 times.

5 **Reasoning** The probability of spinning red on this spinner is $\frac{2}{5}$.
Luca spins it 100 times.
He calculates the expected number of times it will land on red:
$100 \div 5 = 20$ $20 \times 2 = 40$
Use Luca's method to calculate the expected number of times it will land on red if he spins it

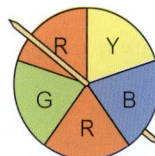

a 200 times   **b** 50 times   **c** 10 times

Calculating probability and expected outcomes

1 On an aeroplane there are two meal choices, vegetarian or chicken.
The airline surveys 100 people to find out how many of each meal to take on each flight.
Of the 100 people, 21 choose vegetarian and the rest choose chicken.

a How many choose chicken?

b Work out

    i P(chicken)   **ii** P(vegetarian)

2 **Problem-solving / Reasoning** In a competition at the school fair, tickets are chosen from a box without looking.
The box contains tickets numbered 1 to 200.
Anyone who picks a ticket that shows a multiple of 10 wins a prize.

a How many multiples of 10 are there between 1 and 200?

b What is the probably of winning? Simplify your answer if possible.

Reflect Will the expected outcome **always** be the same as the actual outcome? Try it – if you roll a dice 6 times do you get each number exactly once? If you did, will this happen every time?

7 Ratio and proportion

7.1 Direct proportion

- Use direct proportion in simple contexts
- Solve simple problems involving direct proportion

Working with one item

1 One brick weighs 3 kg.

= 3 kg

   a Write the multiplication you need to do to find the weight of

   i 2 bricks

   ii 6 bricks

   b Write the weight of:

   i 2 bricks   **ii** 6 bricks

2 One packet of crisps costs 50p. Find the cost of

   a 2 packets

   b 3 packets

3 One textbook costs £7. Find the cost of

   a 10 textbooks   **b** 50 textbooks   **c** 200 textbooks

4 **Reasoning**   Two marbles weigh 30 g.   = 30 g

   a Write the calculation you need to do to find the weight of 1 marble.

   b What is the weight of 1 marble?

5 **Reasoning**   A pair of trainers weighs 400 g.

   a Do you multiply or divide to find the
       weight of 1 trainer?

   b What is the weight of 1 trainer?

> **Q5b hint** Check your answer: If 1 trainer weighs
> ☐ g, then does a pair of trainers weigh 400 g?

6 Ten pencils cost 80p.
    What is the cost of 1 pencil?

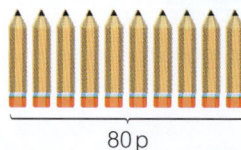

80 p

Working out information about multiple items

Worked example

2 eggs weigh 80 g.
What do 6 eggs weigh?

$80\,g \div 2 = 40\,g$ —— First, divide by 2 to work out what 1 egg weighs.

$40\,g \times 6 = 240\,g$ —— Next, multiply by 6 to work out what 6 eggs weigh.

1 A recipe for 2 people uses 100 g of flour.
   Copy and complete the calculations.
   a For 1 person you need $100 \div 2 = \square$ g of flour
   b For 5 people you need $\square \times 5 = \square$ g of flour.

2 Four bicycle wheels cost £200.
   a What is the cost of 1 wheel?
   b What is the cost of 2 wheels?

   = £200

3 Four tickets to the cinema cost £28.
   a How much is 1 ticket?
   b How much are 5 tickets?

   = £28

4 On holiday Mr Jones exchanges £10 for ¥80 (Japanese yen).
   a How many yen does he get for £1?
   b How many yen does he get for £60?

5 **Problem-solving**   To make 12 gingerbread men you need:
   360 g flour   120 g butter   240 g sugar
   Write how much of each ingredient you need for
   a 1 gingerbread man   b 10 gingerbread men

6 **Problem-solving**   Six pens cost £12.
   What is the cost of 2 pens?

   Q6 hint What calculation might you need to do first?

Reflect   Jenny knows that 12 eggs cost £1.44. How can she work out how much
6 eggs cost? Can you think of more than one way?

7.2 Writing ratios

- Use ratio notation
- Reduce a ratio to its simplest form

Ratios in tile and bead patterns

1 Problem-solving A pattern is made of black and white tiles.

■ □ □ ■ □ □

a Draw the next three tiles in the pattern.

b i How many black tiles did you draw?　　ii How many white tiles did you draw?

c Copy and complete.

For every 1 black tile there are ☐ white tiles.

> **Key point** A ratio is a way of comparing two or more quantities.
> Ratios are written as numbers separated by a colon.
> For example, this tile pattern has 1 black tile and 2 white tiles. ■ □ □
> The ratio of black to white tiles is 1 : 2.

Guided

2 Write the ratio of red to blue tiles for each pattern.

a R B B B

red : blue = 1 : ☐

b R B B B B B

red : blue = ☐ : ☐

c R R B

red : blue = 2 : ☐

d R R R B B

red : blue = ☐ : ☐

Guided

3 Write the ratio of green to yellow tiles for each pattern.

a G Y Y G Y

green : yellow = 2 : ☐

b G G Y G Y G

green : yellow = ☐ : ☐

c G G Y G Y G Y

green : yellow = ☐ : ☐

d Y Y G Y Y Y

green : yellow = ☐ : ☐

4 Problem-solving The ratio of grey to white tiles in a pattern is 1 : 4.

Sarah draws the ratio like this: □ □ ▨ □ □

a Draw this ratio in two ways that are different from what Sarah has drawn.

b How did you know how many tiles to draw in total?

5 Problem-solving There are 3 blue beads for every 5 yellow beads on a necklace. Write the ratio of blue : yellow.

> **Q5 hint** You could draw the blue beads and the yellow beads to help you.

Simplifying ratios

Key point   You can simplify a ratio by dividing the numbers in the ratio by the same number.

1 Copy and complete the calculations to write each ratio in its simplest form.

a   2 : 6
÷2 (   ) ÷2
1 : ☐

b   10 : 14
÷2 (   ) ÷2
☐ : ☐

c   4 : 10
÷2 (   ) ÷☐
☐ : ☐

d   3 : 9
÷3 (   ) ÷3
☐ : ☐

e   10 : 15
÷5 (   ) ÷5
☐ : ☐

f   6 : 9
÷3 (   ) ÷☐
☐ : ☐

2 Write the ratio of purple beads to white beads for each necklace.
Simplify the ratio, if possible. The first one has been started for you.

a
purple : white = 3 : 6
= 1 : ☐

b
purple : white = ☐ : ☐
= ☐ : ☐

c
purple : white = ☐ : ☐
= ☐ : ☐

Key point   You can write a ratio in its **simplest form** by dividing the numbers in the ratio by their highest common factor.

3 Simplify each ratio by dividing each part of the ratio by the highest common factor.
The first one has been done for you.

Ratio	Highest common factor	Simplified ratio
2 : 4	2	1 : 2
4 : 6	2	2 : ☐
6 : 8	2	☐ : ☐
8 : 10	☐	☐ : ☐
3 : 6	3	☐ : ☐
6 : 9	3	☐ : ☐
9 : 12	☐	☐ : ☐
4 : 8	4	☐ : ☐
8 : 12	4	☐ : ☐
12 : 16	☐	☐ : ☐

Reflect   Jeremy says: 'Knowing my times tables really helps when simplifying ratios.'
Did knowing your times tables help you to simplify ratios? What other maths skills did you use?

7.3 Using ratios

- Divide a quantity into two parts in a given ratio
- Solve word problems involving ratio

Equivalent ratios

> **Key point** Multiplying all the numbers in a ratio by the same number gives an **equivalent ratio**.

1 Copy and complete to find equivalent ratios.

  a
  $5:1$
  $\times 2 \big(\quad \big) \times 2$
  $\square:2$

  b
  $6:5$
  $\times 3 \big(\quad \big) \times 3$
  $18:\square$

  c
  $3:2$
  $\times 10 \big(\quad \big) \times 10$
  $\square:\square$

2 a Copy and complete these equivalent ratios to $1:3$.

  i
  $1:3$
  $\times 2 \big(\quad \big) \times 2$
  $\square:6$

  ii
  $1:3$
  $\times 3 \big(\quad \big) \times 3$
  $3:\square$

  iii
  $1:3$
  $\times 4 \big(\quad \big) \times 4$
  $\square:\square$

  > **Q2 hint** Multiply both parts of the ratio by the same number.

  b **Problem-solving** Write three other equivalent ratios to $1:3$.

  c **Reasoning** For part **b**, one of Freddie's answers is $11:33$. Is this correct? Show working to explain.

3 Each of these ratios has an equivalent ratio. Match the pairs.

  $1:2$ $8:12$ $15:20$ $3:1$ $9:3$
  $2:3$ $7:14$ $3:4$ $21:6$
  $7:2$

Guided

4 Abbie works out an equivalent ratio to $3:5$. The second number in Abbie's equivalent ratio has been rubbed out.

  > **Q4 hint** $3 \times \square = 6$

  $3:5$
  $\times \square \big(\quad \big) \times \square$
  $6:$ ▨

  a What has Abbie multiplied 3 by to give 6?

  b What should Abbie multiply 5 by?

  c What is the number that has been rubbed out?

5 Copy and complete the equivalent ratios.

  a $1:5 = 2:\square$ b $1:6 = 2:\square$ c $1:7 = 2:\square$

  d $1:5 = 3:\square$ e $1:6 = 3:\square$ f $1:7 = 3:\square$

  g $2:3 = 4:\square$ h $2:3 = 6:\square$ i $2:3 = 8:\square$

Using equivalent ratios to solve problems

Guided

1 Alex makes necklaces. In every necklace the ratio of black beads to red beads is 1 : 2.

   a Copy and complete the table showing the number of beads in different length necklaces.

Necklace	Number of black beads	Number of red beads
●●●	1	2
●●●●●●	☐	☐
●●●●●●●●●	☐	☐
●●●●●●●●●●●●	☐	☐

   b i Copy and complete the ratio to work out how many red beads Alex will need if he uses 8 black beads.

   Black : Red
   1 : 2
   ×8 ⟨ ⟩ ×8
   8 : ☐

   ii How many beads does Alex need in total?

Worked example

The ratio of cows to sheep in a field is 2 : 3.

There are 20 cows in the field.

a How many sheep are there?

   cows : sheep
   2 : 3
   ×10 ⟨ ⟩ ×10 ——— The number of cows is multiplied by 10.
   20 : 30   Therefore multiply the number of sheep by 10.

There are 30 sheep in the field.

b What is the total number of animals in the field?

   20 + 30 = 50 ——— There are 20 cows and 30 sheep. Add them to find the total number of animals.

There are 50 animals in the field.

Guided

2 The ratio of adults to children on a bus is 1 : 6.

   Copy and complete the calculations to work out how many children are on the bus when there are

   a 2 adults

   adults : children
   1 : 6
   ×2 ⟨ ⟩ ×2
   2 : ☐

   b 3 adults

   adults : children
   1 : 6
   ×3 ⟨ ⟩ ×☐
   ☐ : ☐

   c 7 adults

   adults : children
   1 : 6
   ×☐ ⟨ ⟩ ×☐
   ☐ : ☐

   d Problem-solving   On Friday, there is a total of 49 people on the bus.

   i How many are adults?

   ii How many are children?

   Q2d hint Look at your answers to a, b and c.
   You are looking for:
   number of adults + number of children = 49

3 The ratio of red counters to blue counters required for a game is 2 : 3.

Copy and complete the calculations to work out how many blue counters are required if there are

a 4 red counters

red : blue
2 : 3

×2 ⤸ ⤷ ×2

4 : ☐   = ☐ blue counters

b 6 red counters

red : blue
2 : 3

×3 ⤸ ⤷ ×☐

☐ : ☐   = ☐ blue counters

c 8 red counters

red : blue
2 : 3

×☐ ⤸ ⤷ ×☐

☐ : ☐   = ☐ blue counters

4 The game in **Q3** is played three times with different numbers of counters.

   a **Problem-solving** In one game, 10 counters are used.

     i How many are red counters?

     ii How many are blue counters?

> **Q4a hint** number of red counters + number of blue counters = 10

   b **Problem-solving** In a second game, 20 counters are used.

     i How many are red counters?

     ii How many are blue counters?

   c **Problem-solving** In a third game, 25 counters are used.

     i How many are red counters?

     ii How many are blue counters?

> **Q4c hint** Try to find different equivalent ratios until the two parts of your ratio (red + blue) add to 25.
>
> red : blue
> 2 : 3
>
> ×☐ ⤸ ⤷ ×☐
>
> ☐ : ☐
>
> ☐ + ☐ = 25

5 **Problem-solving** The ratio of white mugs to green mugs on a shelf is 1 : 3.

There are 12 mugs in total. How many are green?

> **Q5 hint**
>
> white : green
> 1 : 3
>
> ×☐ ⤸ ⤷ ×☐
>
> ☐ : ☐
>
> ☐ + ☐ = 12

Reflect Write the ratio of adults to children in your classroom.

Add the parts of your ratio. What does this tell you?

7.4 Ratios, proportions and fractions

- Use fractions to describe proportions
- Understand the relationship between ratio and proportion

Proportions as fractions

Key point   A proportion compares a part with a whole. It can be written as a fraction.

1 Write the proportion of each bar that is yellow.
The first one has been started for you.

a

$$\text{proportion of yellow} = \frac{\text{number of yellow parts}}{\text{total number of parts (whole)}} = \frac{\square}{5}$$

b

c

d

> **Q1c hint** proportion of yellow = $\frac{\square}{7}$

2 Write the proportion of each circle that is red. Simplify the fractions.

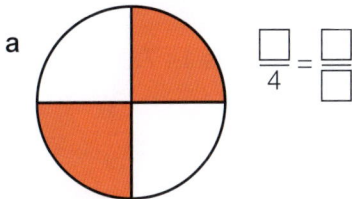

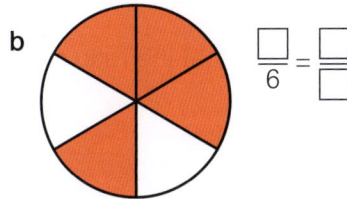

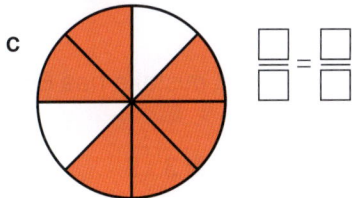

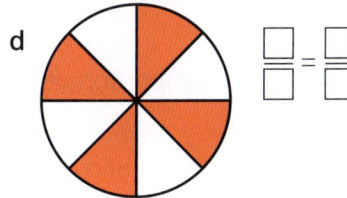

a $\frac{\square}{4} = \frac{\square}{\square}$

b $\frac{\square}{6} = \frac{\square}{\square}$

c $\frac{\square}{\square} = \frac{\square}{\square}$

d $\frac{\square}{\square} = \frac{\square}{\square}$

3 Here are 7 counters.

O O O B B B B

Write the proportion that are
a orange   b blue

4 A box contains 2 white balls and 5 black balls.
   a What proportion of the balls are white?
   b What proportion of the balls are black?

> **Q4 hint** Draw a picture to help you.

Ratios and proportions as fractions

1 **a** Write the ratio of blue to red tiles in
the pattern.

B	B	R	R	R

blue : red = 2 : ☐

b Copy and complete.

  i The proportion of blue tiles = $\frac{\Box}{5}$

  ii The proportion of red tiles = $\frac{\Box}{5}$

2 These are Omar's pet rabbits and mice.

a Write the ratio of rabbits to mice.
b What proportion of Omar's pets are rabbits?
c What proportion of Omar's pets are mice?

3 The bar needs to be shaded so that the ratio of green to black tiles is 1 : 7.

a Copy and shade the bar.
b Write the proportion of the bar that is:
  i green   **ii** black
c **Reasoning** Ed writes that the proportion of green tiles is $\frac{1}{7}$. What mistake has Ed made?

4 This circle is to be coloured so that the ratio of blue to red segments is 3 : 5.

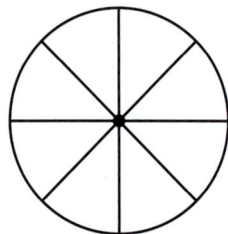

a What proportion of the circle will be coloured red?
b What proportion of the circle will be coloured blue?

7.5 Proportions and percentages

- Use percentages to describe proportions
- Use percentages to compare simple proportions
- Understand the relationship between ratio and proportion

Proportions as percentages

Key point A proportion compares a part with a whole. It can be written as a percentage.

Guided

1 Copy and complete to write these fractions as percentages.

a ×10

$$\frac{1}{10} = \frac{10}{100} = \boxed{}\%$$

×10

b ×2

$$\frac{2}{50} = \frac{\boxed{}}{100} = \boxed{}\%$$

×2

c ×10

$$\frac{7}{10} = \frac{\boxed{}}{100} = \boxed{}\%$$

×10

d ×☐

$$\frac{6}{20} = \frac{\boxed{}}{100} = \boxed{}\%$$

×5

e ×☐

$$\frac{4}{25} = \frac{\boxed{}}{100} = \boxed{}\%$$

×4

f ×☐

$$\frac{3}{5} = \frac{\boxed{}}{\boxed{}} = \boxed{}\%$$

×☐

2 Use the method in **Q1** to write these fractions as percentages.

a $\frac{41}{100}$ b $\frac{7}{50}$ c $\frac{3}{10}$

d $\frac{9}{20}$ e $\frac{7}{25}$ f $\frac{2}{5}$

3 The proportion of people who own a computer is $\frac{87}{100}$.
   What percentage is this?

4 The proportion of people who buy their music online is $\frac{21}{50}$.
   Write this as a percentage.

5 **Problem-solving** In a group of 100 students, 51 are boys.
   Write the proportion of boys as
   a a fraction   b a percentage

6 **Problem-solving** There are 10 sweets in a bag.
   9 of them are strawberry flavour.
   Write the proportion of strawberry sweets as
   a a fraction   b a percentage

10 sweets

> **Key point** You can compare proportions using percentages.

7 Problem-solving Ali and Tom work together.

a Ali works 50 hours a week. She spends 22 hours at her desk.
Write this proportion as
  i a fraction   **ii** a percentage

b Tom works 25 hours a week. He spends 15 hours at his desk.
Write this proportion as
  i a fraction   **ii** a percentage

c Who spends the greatest proportion of their work time at a desk: Ali or Tom?

> **Q7c hint** Which percentage is greater: Ali's percentage time at her desk or Tom's percentage time at his desk?

Ratios and proportions as percentages

1 a Write the ratio of blue to red tiles in the pattern.

| B | B | B | R | R | R | R | R | R | R |

blue : red = 3 : ☐

> **Q1a hint**
> number of blue tiles : number of red tiles

b Copy and complete.

  i proportion of blue tiles $= \frac{\square}{10} = \frac{\square}{100} = \square\%$

  ii proportion of red tiles $= \frac{\square}{10} = \frac{\square}{100} = \square\%$

2 Here are some shapes.

■ ■ ■ ■ ■ ■ ■ ■ ■ ■ ● ● ● ● ● ● ● ● ● ●

a Write the ratio of squares to circles.

b What proportion of the shapes are squares? Give your answer as a percentage.

c What proportion of the shapes are circles? Give your answer as a percentage.

> **Q2b hint** proportion of squares $= \frac{\square}{20} = \frac{\square}{100} = \square\%$

Guided

3 The bar needs to be shaded so that the ratio of grey to white tiles is 2 : 3.

| | | | | |

a Copy and shade the bar.

b Write the proportion of the bar that is
  i grey   **ii** white
Give your answers as percentages.

> **Reflect** Is it easier to write proportion as a percentage or a fraction?
> Does your answer depend on the total number of objects?

8 Lines and angles

8.1 Measuring and drawing angles

• Use a protractor to measure and draw angles

Measuring angles

Key point A protractor has two scales that both start at 0° but go in opposite directions. You can use them to measure and draw acute angles (smaller than 90°) and obtuse angles (greater than 90°).

70°   110°

Worked example

Measure these angles.

a 120°

b 30°

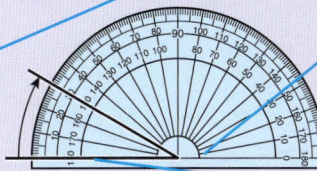

Place the ☼ at the centre of the protractor on the vertex of the angle.

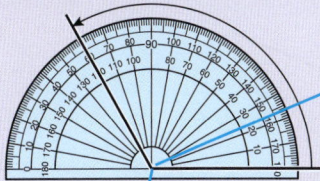

vertex (point) of the angle

Line up the zero line with one line of the angle, and read up from 0° to the other line.

1 What angles are these protractors measuring?

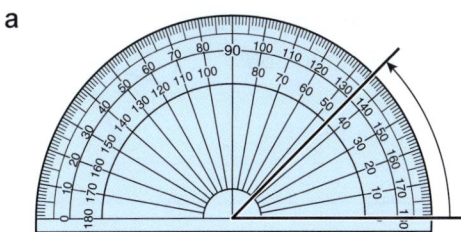

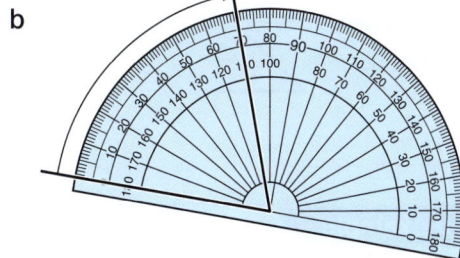

a

b

2 Measure each angle.

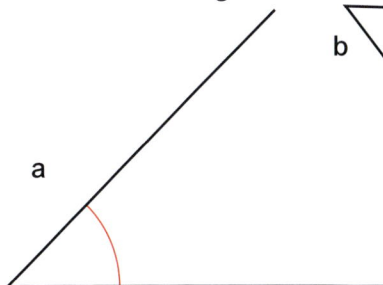

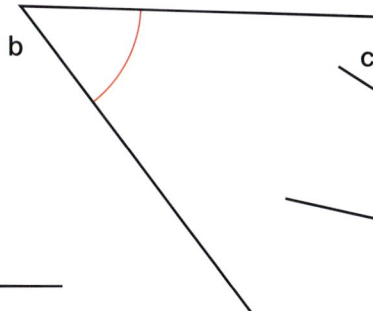

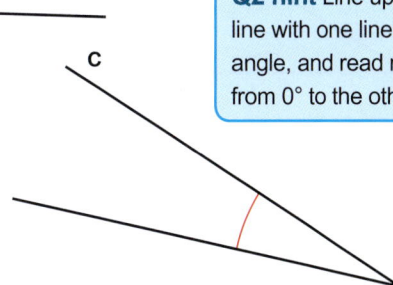

b

c

a

Q2 hint Line up the zero line with one line of the angle, and read round from 0° to the other line.

3 These angles are larger than 90°.
What angles are these protractors measuring?

a

b

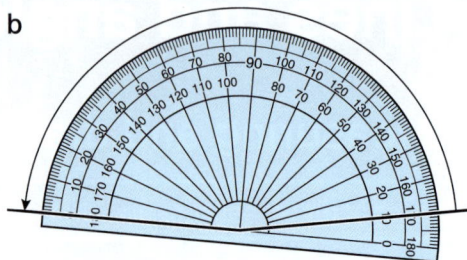

4 **Problem-solving** Measure these angles.

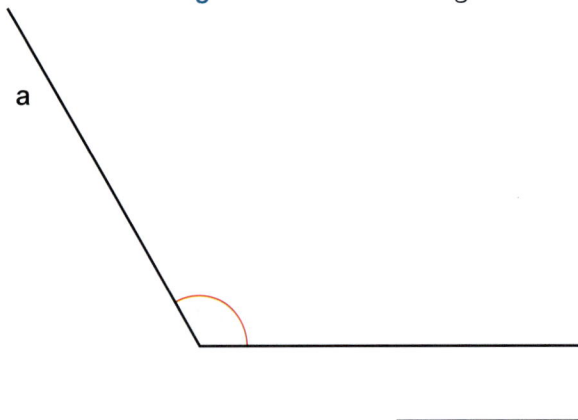

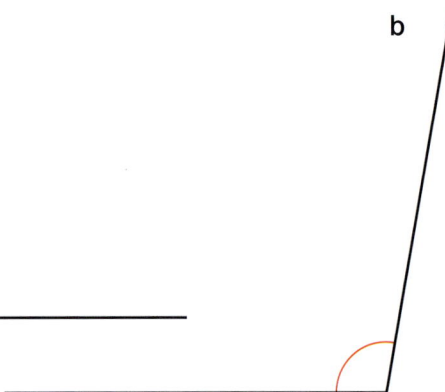

a

b

c

Q4 hint Make sure you use the correct scale. Line up the zero line with one line of the angle, and read round from 0° to the other line.

Key point

A whole turn is 360°.

An **obtuse** angle is between 90° and 180°.

An **acute** angle is smaller than 90°.

A **reflex** angle is more than 180° but less than 360°.

Worked example

Measure angle a.

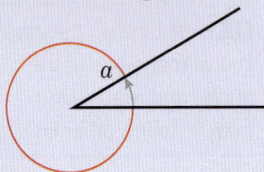

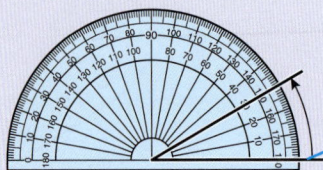

Measure the smaller angle first. There are 360° in a full turn so the reflex angle is
360° − smaller angle

The acute angle is 30°.
The reflex angle is 360° − 30° = 330°

5 Measure these reflex angles. One has been started for you.

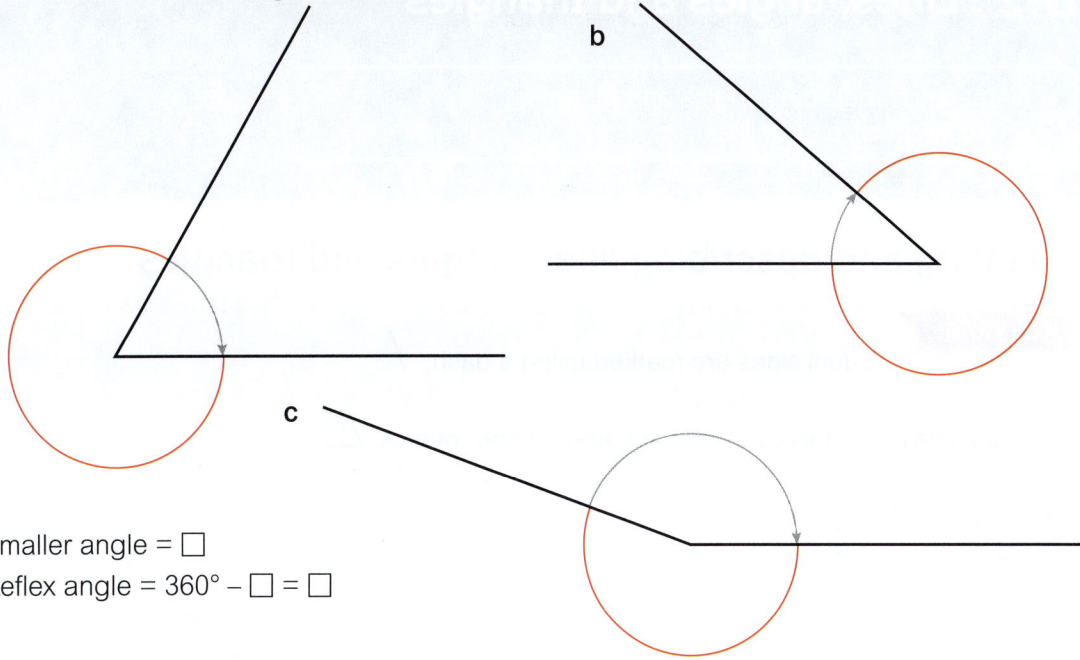

a

b

c

Smaller angle = ☐
Reflex angle = 360° − ☐ = ☐

Drawing angles

1 Follow these instructions to draw an angle of 50°.

    a Use a ruler to draw a straight line about 6 cm long.

    b Place your protractor so the 🔆 is at the
       left end of your straight line.

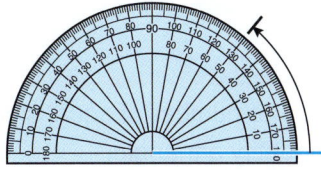

    c Start at 0° and read up to 50°. Mark the point.

    d Use your ruler to join the left end of your straight line to your mark.

2 Follow these instructions to draw an angle of 65°.

    a Use a ruler to draw a straight line about 6 cm long.

    b Place your protractor so the 🔆 is at the left end of your straight line.

    c Start at 0° and read up to 65°. Mark the point.

    d Use your ruler to join the left end of your straight line to your mark.

Reflect   Sam uses a protractor in this way to
measure the angle. What mistake has Sam made?

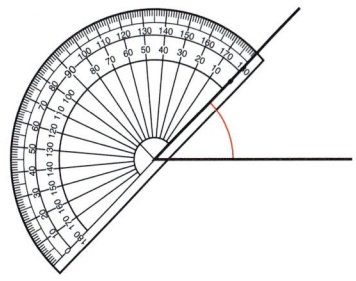

8.2 Lines, angles and triangles

- Name and label lines, angles and triangles
- Estimate the size of angles

Naming and describing lines, angles and triangles

> **Key point**
> Equal sides are marked using a dash.
>
> Equal angles are marked using the same number of arcs.

1 For each triangle

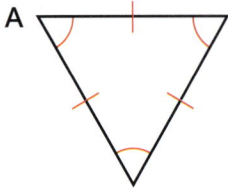

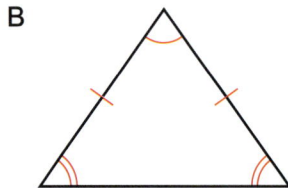

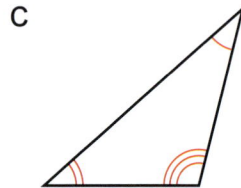

A

B

C

   a write how many equal sides it has

   b write how many equal angles it has

> **Q1a hint** How many sides are marked with dashes?

> **Q1b hint** How many angles have the same number of arcs?

> **Key point**
> The number of equal sides and equal angles can help you identify a triangle.
>
> **scalene**   **isosceles**   **equilateral**
>
> all angles and sides different   two equal angles and sides   all angles and sides equal

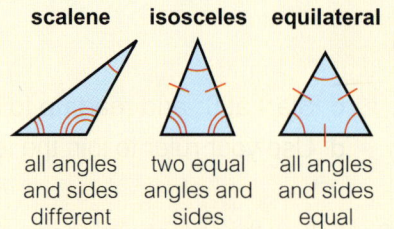

2 Name the triangles in **Q1**.

3 Match each triangle to the correct name from the box.

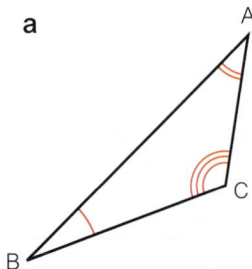

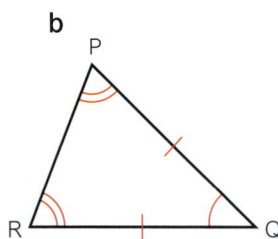

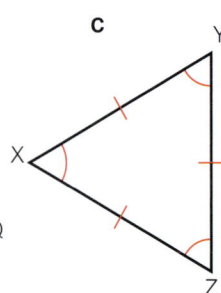

a A, C, B

b P, R, Q

c Y, X, Z

equilateral   isosceles   scalene

4 Triangle PQR has sides PQ, QR and PR.

    a Which side is equal to PQ?

    b Which side is not equal to PQ?

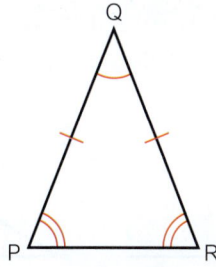

5 Triangle ABC has angles ABC, BAC and ACB.

    a Which angle is equal to ABC?

    b Which angles are not equal to ACB?

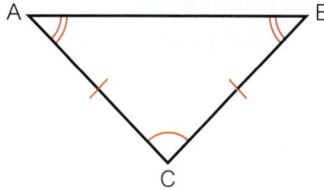

Key point

Perpendicular lines meet at **right angles** (90°). This symbol means the angle is a right angle.

Parallel lines are always the same distance apart and never meet. Lines that are parallel are represented by arrows.

---

6 Look at these pairs of lines. Are they perpendicular, parallel or neither?
Copy the parallel lines and mark them with arrows.
Copy the perpendicular lines and mark them with a right angle symbol.

  a    **b**    **c** 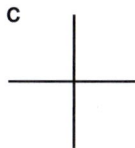   **d**

  e    **f**    **g**    **h**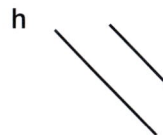

7 Look at these shapes.
Write the number of pairs of parallel lines in each shape.

  a 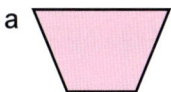   **b** 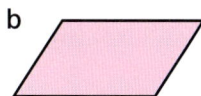   **c**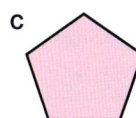

  d 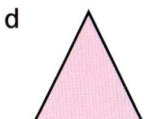   **e**    **f**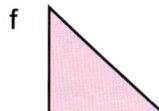

Estimating angles

1 Here are some angles.

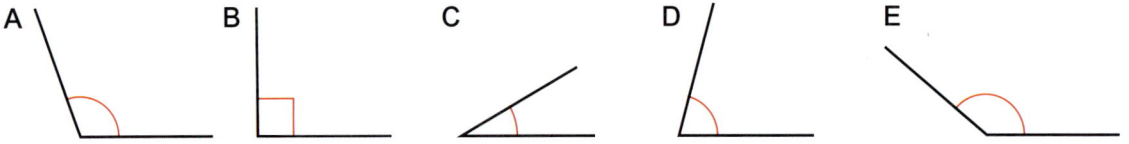

A   B   C   D   E

    a Which angles are smaller than 90°?

    b Which angles are larger than 90°?

    c **Reasoning** Which angle do you estimate to be 100°?

> **Q1c hint** Is it larger or smaller than 90°? How close is it to 90°?

2 This angle is 45°. It is half a right angle.

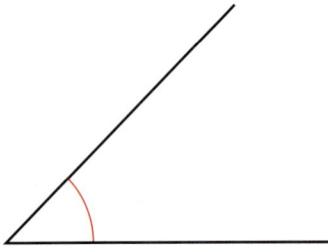

    Look at the angles below.

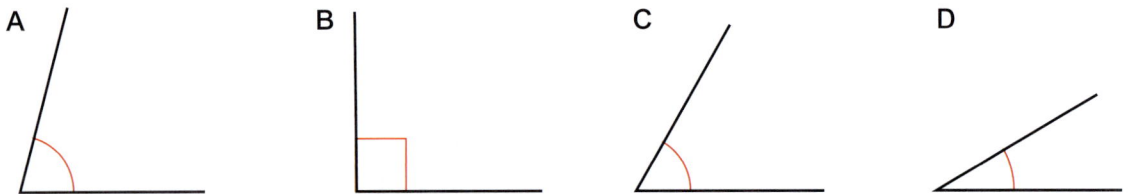

A   B   C   D

    a Which angles are smaller than 45°?

    b Which angles are larger than 45°?

3 **Problem-solving** Choose the best estimate for each of these angles.

    a

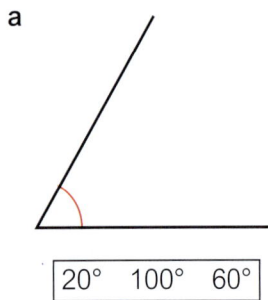

    | 20°   100°   60° |

    b

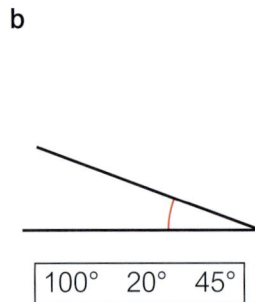

    | 100°   20°   45° |

    c

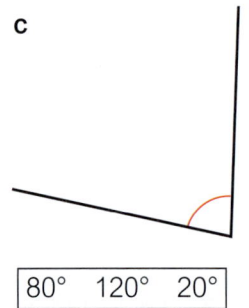

    | 80°   120°   20° |

> **Reflect**   Is it possible to draw a triangle with two parallel sides? Is it possible to draw a triangle with two perpendicular sides?

• Use a ruler and protractor to draw triangles accurately

Drawing triangles accurately, with two sides and one angle given

1 Copy this sketch of triangle ABC.

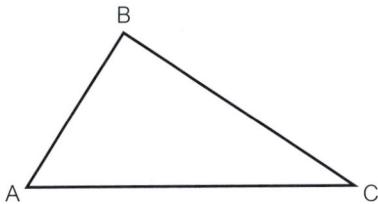

> **Q1 hint** When sketching triangles, you do not have to draw them accurately.

a Label side AB: 5 cm
b Label side BC: 7 cm
c Label side AC: 8 cm
d Label angle BAC: 50°

2 Use a ruler to draw each of these lines accurately.
a 5 cm
b 8 cm
c 6.5 cm

3 Use a protractor to draw each of these angles accurately.
a 50°
b 90°
c 65°

4 Follow these steps to draw this triangle accurately.

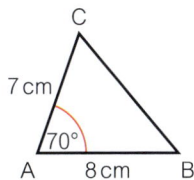

a Use a ruler to draw a line of 8 cm. Label the line AB.

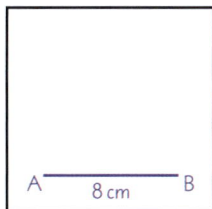

b Place your protractor so the ▨ is at A. Mark the angle at 70°. Draw a long line from A through your 70° mark.

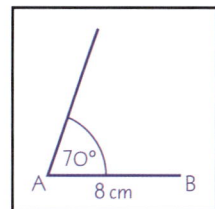

c Measure your long line and mark where it is 7 cm. Label this C.

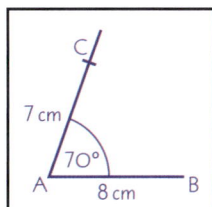

d Join BC to give the third side of your triangle.

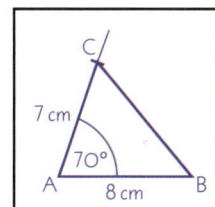

5 Use a ruler and protractor to draw these triangles accurately.

Q5 hint Follow similar steps to **Q4**.

a

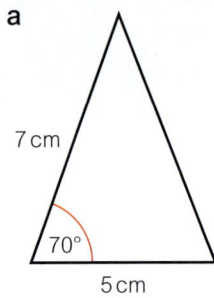

7 cm

70°

5 cm

b

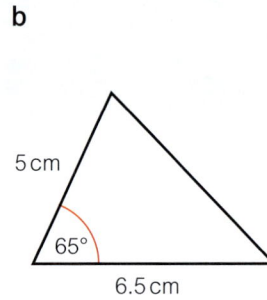

5 cm

65°

6.5 cm

Drawing triangles accurately, with two angles and one side given

1 Follow these steps to draw this triangle accurately.

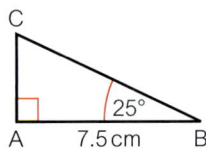

C

25°

A   7.5 cm   B

a Use a ruler to draw a line of 7.5 cm. Label the line AB.

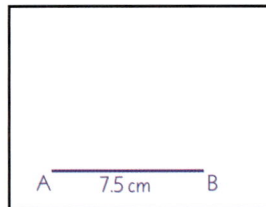

A   7.5 cm   B

b Place your protractor so the ☼ is at A. Mark the angle at 90°. Draw a long line from A through your 90° mark.

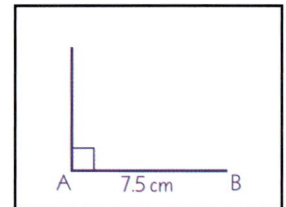

A   7.5 cm   B

c Place your protractor so the ☼ is at B. Mark the angle at 25°. Draw a long line from B through your 25° mark until it crosses the line from A. Label this point C.

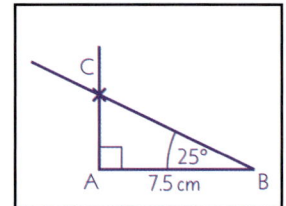

C

25°

A   7.5 cm   B

2 Use a ruler and protractor to draw these triangles accurately.

Q2 hint Follow similar steps to **Q1**.

a

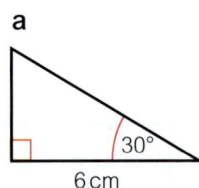

30°

6 cm

b

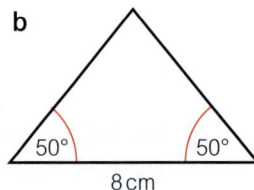

50°   50°

8 cm

c

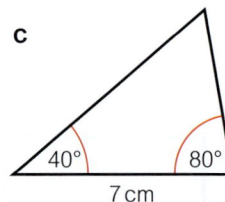

40°   80°

7 cm

> **Reflect**   Gaby says: 'You should always use a sharp pencil when drawing triangles.'
> Why do you think this is important?

8.4 Calculating angles

- Use the rules for angles on a straight line, angles around a point and vertically opposite angles

Angles on a straight line

Guided

1 Work out
- **a** 180 – 60
- **b** 180 – 100
- **c** 180 – 120
- **d** 180 – 90
- **e** 180 – 80
- **f** 180 – 45

2 Write the two angles measured on each straight line. The first one has been started for you.

a

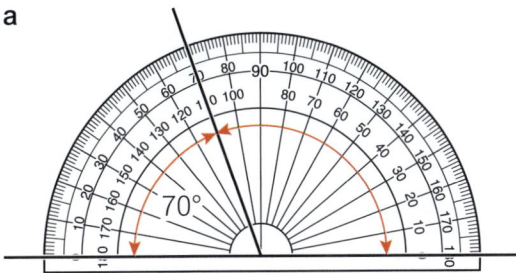

70°

b

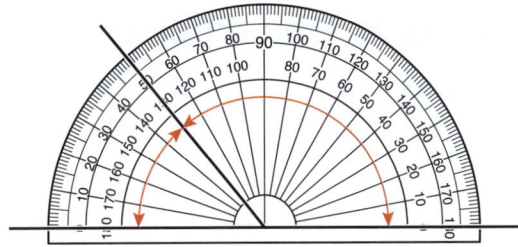

c

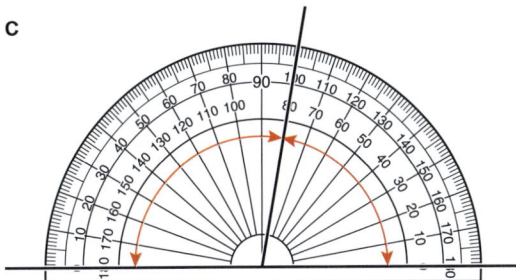

d

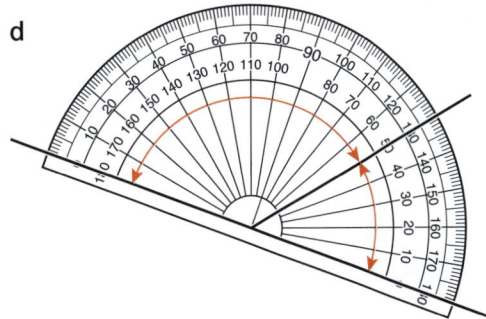

3 Add together each pair of angles in **Q2**. What do you notice?

> **Key point**
>
> The angles on a straight line add up to 180°.
>
>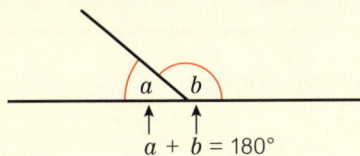
>
> $a + b = 180°$

> **Worked example**
>
> Find angle b.
>
> $40 + b = 180$
>
> $b = 180 - 40$
>
> $b = 140°$
>
>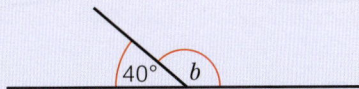
>
> 40° b

4 Work out the size of each unknown angle.

a

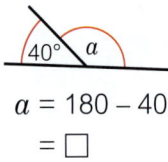

$a = 180 - 40$
$= \square$

b

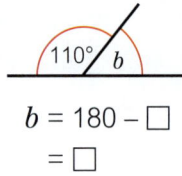

$b = 180 - \square$
$= \square$

c

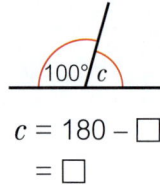

$c = 180 - \square$
$= \square$

d

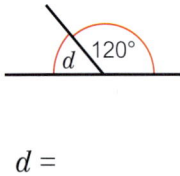

$d =$

e

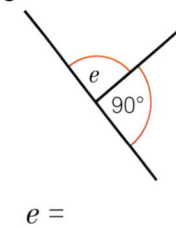

$e =$

f

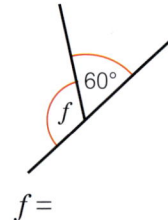

$f =$

Angles around a point

1 Work out

a $360 - 60$ **b** $360 - 100$ **c** $360 - 120$

d $360 - 90$ **e** $360 - 180$ **f** $360 - 240$

Key point

The angles around a point add up to 360°.

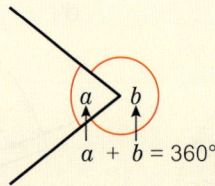

$a + b = 360°$

Worked example

Find angle a.

$290 + a = 360$
$a = 360 - 290$
$a = 70°$

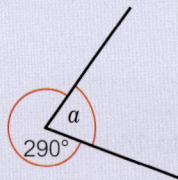

2 Work out the size of each unknown angle.

a

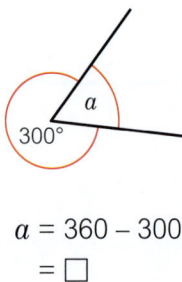

$a = 360 - 300$
$= \square$

b

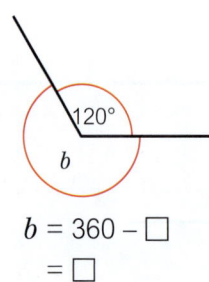

$b = 360 - \square$
$= \square$

c

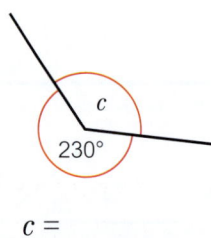

$c =$

d

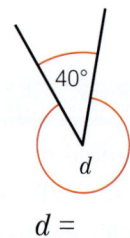

$d =$

Vertically opposite angles

Key point   When two straight lines cross, the angles opposite each other are equal.
They are called **vertically opposite angles**.

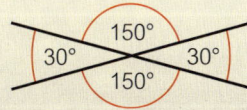

Worked example

Work out the size of the unknown angle.

$x = 140°$

140° and x are vertically opposite angles.

---

1 Work out the size of each unknown angle.

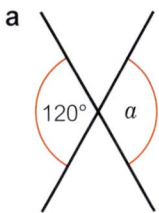

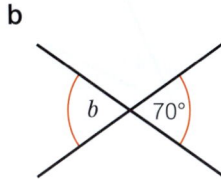

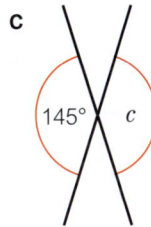

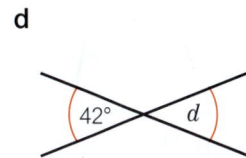

a   120° a

b b 70°

c   145° c

d   42° d

---

2 **Problem-solving**

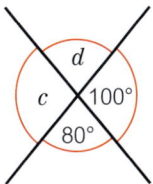

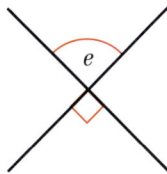

d
c 100°
80°

e

a Which angle is vertically opposite to c?   b What is the size of angle c?
c Which angle is vertically opposite to d?   d What is the size of angle d?
e Which angle is vertically opposite to e?   f What is the size of angle e?

---

3 **Problem-solving**   Work out the size of each unknown angle.

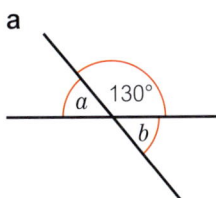

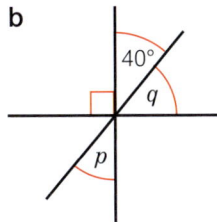

a a 130°
      b

b   40°
      q
      p

Q3a hint Angles on a straight line add up to 180°.
$a + 130° = 180°$
$a = 180 - 130 = \square$

Q3b hint $90° + 40° = \square$

Reflect   Copy and complete each sentence with one of the options in the box.

a Angles on a straight line add up to _____
b Vertically opposite angles are _____
c Angles around a point add up to _____

| 360°   180°   equal |

8.5 Angles in a triangle

- Use the rule for the sum of angles in a triangle
- Calculate exterior angles

Missing interior angles in a triangle

1 Add up the angles in each triangle.

a 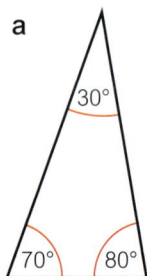 **b** 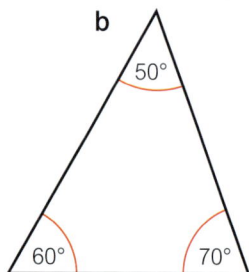 **c**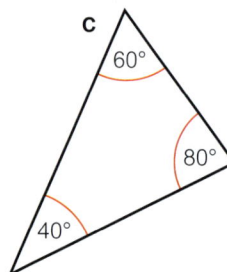

d Reasoning What do you notice?

> **Key point** Angles in a triangle add up to 180°.

> **Worked example**
>
> Work out the size of angle x.
>
> $x = 180° - 130° - 25°$ ——— Subtract the angles you know from 180°.
>
> $= 25°$

Guided

2 Work out the size of angle x in each triangle.

a 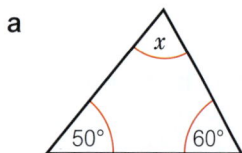 **b** 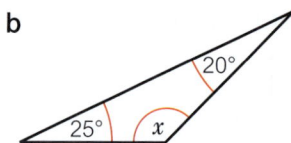 **c**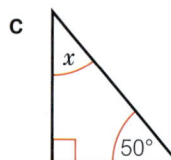

$x = 180° - 50° - 60°$ $x = 180° - 25° - 20°$ $x = 180° - 90° - 50°$

$= \square$ $= \square$ $= \square$

Guided

3 Work out the size of the missing angle in each of these triangles. One has been started for you.

a 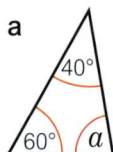 **b** 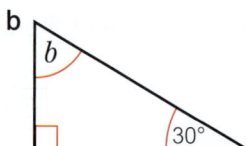 **c**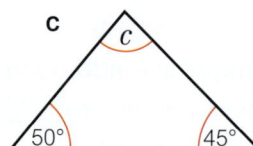

$a = 180° - \square - \square = \square$

Missing exterior angles in a triangle

1 Add together the given angles in each diagram.

a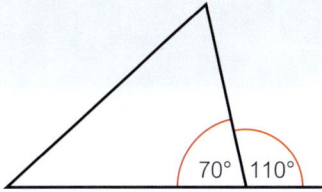

b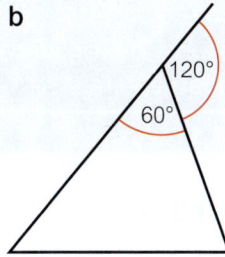

c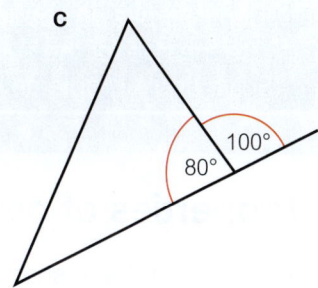

b Reasoning What do you notice?

> **Key point** An **interior angle** is inside a shape.
> An **exterior angle** is outside the shape on a straight line next to the interior angle.
> interior angle + exterior angle = 180°
>
>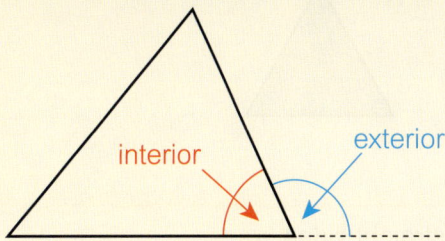

2 Work out the exterior angle in each of these triangles.

Q2 hint Angles on a straight line add up to 180°.

a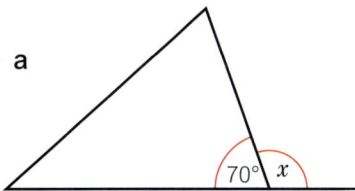

$x = 180° - 70°$
$= \square$

b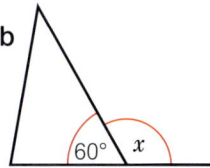

$x = 180° - \square$
$= \square$

c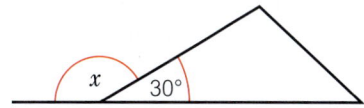

$x = 180° - \square$
$= \square$

> **Reflect** William says: 'Interior angles are on the inside of a shape and exterior angles are on the outside.'
> Write a better definition, in your own words, of interior angles.
> Then write a definition of exterior angles.
> Draw diagrams to help with your explanations.

8.6 Quadrilaterals

- Identify types of quadrilateral
- Use the rule for the sum of angles in a quadrilateral
- Solve angle problems involving quadrilaterals

Properties of quadrilaterals

1 Which of these shapes are quadrilaterals?

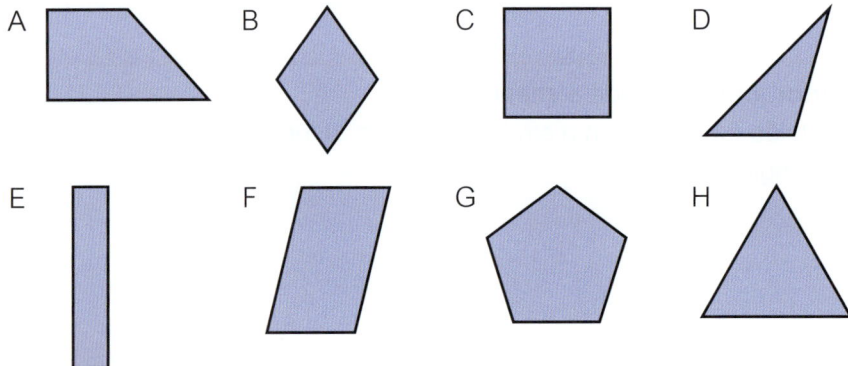

A   B   C   D

E   F   G   H

> **Key point** A **quadrilateral** is a 2D (flat) shape with 4 straight sides.

2 Choose the properties of each shape from the cloud. Each shape can have more than one property. The first one has been started for you.

a square   A, ___, ___

b rectangle

c parallelogram

d rhombus

e isosceles trapezium

f trapezium

g kite

> A – has two pairs of parallel sides
> B – has one pair of parallel sides
> C – has no right angles
> D – has four right angles
> E – all sides have equal length
> F – opposite sides have equal length
> G – opposite angles are equal

Calculating missing angles in a quadrilateral

1 Work out the sum of the angles in each of these quadrilaterals.

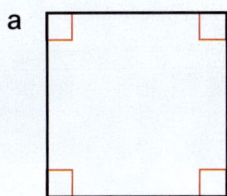

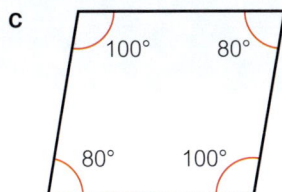

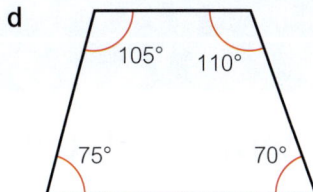

a

b

c

d

2 Copy and complete the statement:
'Angles in a quadrilateral add up to ☐°.'

3 **Reasoning** Reece is trying to draw a quadrilateral with four angles each measuring 100°. Why can't he draw it?

Guided

4 Here is a kite. You need to find angle a.

a Type 360 into your calculator.

b Subtract the angles from this quadrilateral, one at a time.
Copy and complete the calculation.
$360 - 92 - 92 - ☐ = ☐$

c When you have subtracted the other angles from 360 you are left with a.
$a = ☐°$

5 **Problem-solving** Use the method in **Q4** to work out the size of the missing angle in each of these quadrilaterals.

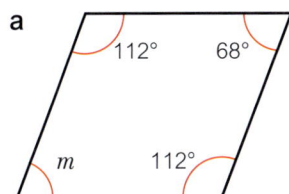

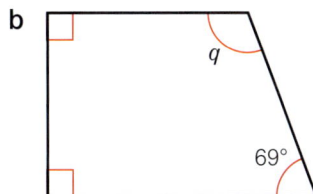

a

b

Reflect Two of the angles in a quadrilateral are larger than 90°. What do you know about the other two angles? Can there be three angles larger than 90°?

9 Sequences and graphs

9.1 Sequences

- Recognise, describe and continue number sequences
- Generate terms of a sequence using a one-step term-to-term rule
- Find missing terms in a sequence

Number sequence terms and rules

Key point   A number **sequence** is a set of numbers. Each number in a sequence is called a **term**.

1   Here is a sequence.

2, 6, 10, 14, 18, ...
↑
first term

The first term is 2. Write

a the second term   **b** the third term   **c** the fourth term   **d** the fifth term

2   For each sequence, write
   i the first term
   ii the third term
   a 1, 11, 21, 31, ...   **b** 3, 7, 11, 15, ...   **c** 65, 60, 55, 50, ...   **d** 24, 20, 16, 12, ...

Key point   A number sequence always follows a **rule**.

Guided

3   Write the rule for each number sequence. The first one has been done for you.
   a 1, 3, 5, 7, ...   **b** 1, 4, 7, 10, ...   **c** 5, 10, 15, 20, ...

   +2 +2 +2
   1   3   5   7   rule:
                      +2

Guided

4   Write the rule for each number sequence. The first one has been done for you.
   a 12, 10, 8, 6, ...   **b** 25, 20, 15, 10, ...   **c** 14, 11, 8, 5, ...

   −2 −2 −2
   12 10 8   6   rule:
                      −2

5 You are given the first term and the rule for each of these sequences.
Write the second and third terms.

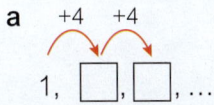

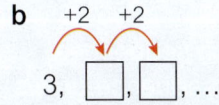

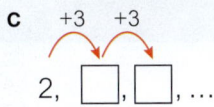

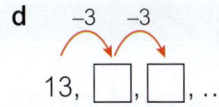

a   +4   +4

1, ☐, ☐, ...

b   +2   +2

3, ☐, ☐, ...

c   +3   +3

2, ☐, ☐, ...

d   −3   −3

13, ☐, ☐, ...

6 Look at the numbers in each sequence. Are they increasing (getting bigger) or decreasing (getting smaller)?

a 10, 9, 8, 7, ...   **b** 11, 21, 31, 41, ...   **c** 8, 17, 26, 35, ...   **d** 100, 75, 50, 25, ...

Number sequence problems

1 Ann has £10 in a jar. Each week she adds £2.
   a How much does she have after 1 week?
   b How much does she have after 2 weeks?
   c How much does she have after 3 weeks?
   d Continue the sequence until you reach £24.
   e How many weeks is it before Ann has £24?

2 **Problem-solving**   John puts £45 in a jar on the first day of the month. Then he takes out £5 to spend that day.
   a How much does he have left in the jar at the end of the first day of the month?
   b On the second day, John takes out and spends another £5. How much does he have left in the jar now?
   c John continues to take out another £5 to spend each day. On what day does John have no money left in his jar?

> **Q2c hint** Write a sequence that shows how much John has in the jar at the end of each day.

Reflect   Eve says: 'Different sequences can have the same first term.'
Write two different sequences with a first term of 3 to show that Eve is correct.
Riz asks: 'Does that mean these sequences share the same rule too?'
Write a sentence in response to Riz.

- Find patterns and rules in sequences
- Describe how a pattern sequence grows

Pattern sequences and rules

> **Key point** A **pattern sequence** is a set of patterns that follow a rule.

Guided

1 Write the rule for each pattern sequence. The first one has been done for you.

a

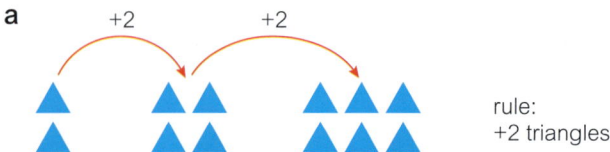

rule:
+2 triangles

b

c

d

2 Each sequence in **Q1** has three patterns.
Draw the fourth pattern for each sequence.

> **Q2 hint** Use the rules you wrote to help you. Look carefully at where the shape or shapes are added in each pattern.

3 Problem-solving Draw the fourth pattern for each of these sequences.

a

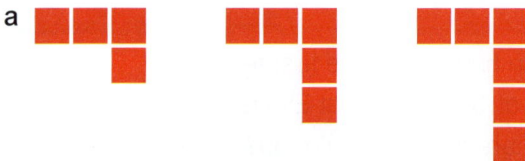

b

c

> **Q3c hint** Look carefully at where shapes are added to each pattern in this sequence.

Using tables for pattern sequences

1 This pattern sequence is made with counters.

Pattern 1   Pattern 2   Pattern 3

There are 4 counters in pattern 1.

a Write the number of counters in
   i pattern 2   **ii** pattern 3
b What is the rule for this pattern sequence?
c Copy and complete this table for the pattern sequence.

Pattern number	1	2	3	4	5
Number of counters	4				

Q1b hint Write how many counters are added each time.

Q1c hint Use the rule you wrote for **c** to work out pattern numbers 4 and 5.

2 This pattern sequence is made with squares.

Pattern 1   Pattern 2   Pattern 3

a Write the number of squares in
   i pattern 1   **ii** pattern 2   **iii** pattern 3
b What is the rule for this pattern sequence?
c Copy and complete this table for the pattern sequence.

Pattern number	1	2	3	4	5
Number of squares					

3 **Problem-solving** This pattern sequence is made with sticks.

Pattern 1   Pattern 2   Pattern 3

a What is the rule for this pattern sequence?
b Copy and complete this table for the pattern sequence:

Pattern number	1	2	3	4	5
Number of sticks					

Q3a hint Look at how many sticks are in patterns 1, 2 and 3. Write how many are added each time.

Reflect   Kinga says: 'It is possible for a pattern sequence to have a subtract rule.'
Draw an example to show that Kinga is correct.
You could start with this pattern made from counters.
Write the rule for your pattern sequence.

9.3 Coordinates and midpoints

- Read and plot coordinates
- Generate and plot coordinates from a rule
- Find the midpoint of a line segment

Reading and plotting coordinates

1 Write the values on these number lines.

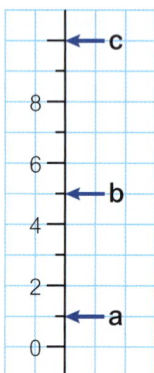

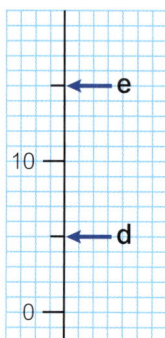

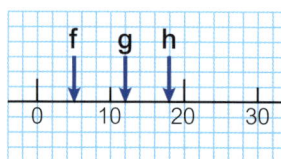

Key point

The x-axis is the horizontal axis.

The x-coordinate is a value on the x-axis.

The y-axis is the vertical axis. The y-coordinate is a value on the y-axis.

The x-coordinate and y-coordinate together tell you where a point is.

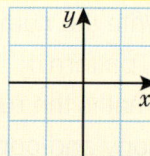

Worked example

Write the coordinates of point A.

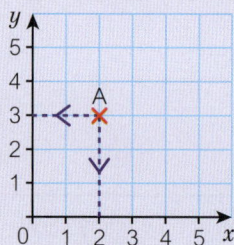

Move down from A (with your finger or a ruler) to the x-axis to find the x-coordinate.

Move across from A (with your finger or a ruler) to the y-axis to find the y-coordinate.

A (2, 3) — Write the x-coordinate first, then a comma, then the y-coordinate.

2 Copy and complete the coordinates of points A, B, C, D and E.

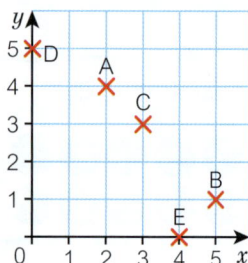

A (2, ☐)   B (☐, 1)

C (3, ☐)   D (☐, 5)

E (☐, ☐)

Using tables for pattern sequences

1 This pattern sequence is made with counters.

Pattern 1   Pattern 2   Pattern 3

There are 4 counters in pattern 1.

a Write the number of counters in

   i pattern 2   **ii** pattern 3

b What is the rule for this pattern sequence?

c Copy and complete this table for the pattern sequence.

Pattern number	1	2	3	4	5
Number of counters	4				

Q1b hint Write how many counters are added each time.

Q1c hint Use the rule you wrote for **c** to work out pattern numbers 4 and 5.

2 This pattern sequence is made with squares.

Pattern 1   Pattern 2   Pattern 3

a Write the number of squares in

   i pattern 1   **ii** pattern 2   **iii** pattern 3

b What is the rule for this pattern sequence?

c Copy and complete this table for the pattern sequence.

Pattern number	1	2	3	4	5
Number of squares					

3 **Problem-solving** This pattern sequence is made with sticks.

Pattern 1   Pattern 2   Pattern 3

a What is the rule for this pattern sequence?

b Copy and complete this table for the pattern sequence:

Pattern number	1	2	3	4	5
Number of sticks					

Q3a hint Look at how many sticks are in patterns 1, 2 and 3. Write how many are added each time.

Reflect   Kinga says: 'It is possible for a pattern sequence to have a subtract rule.'

Draw an example to show that Kinga is correct.

You could start with this pattern made from counters.

Write the rule for your pattern sequence.

9.3 Coordinates and midpoints

- Read and plot coordinates
- Generate and plot coordinates from a rule
- Find the midpoint of a line segment

Reading and plotting coordinates

1 Write the values on these number lines.

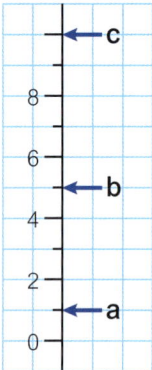

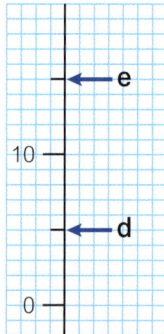

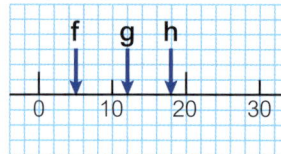

> **Key point** The x-axis is the horizontal axis.
> The x-coordinate is a value on the x-axis.
> The y-axis is the vertical axis. The y-coordinate is a value on the y-axis.
> The x-coordinate and y-coordinate together tell you where a point is.

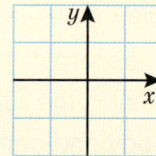

Worked example

Write the coordinates of point A.

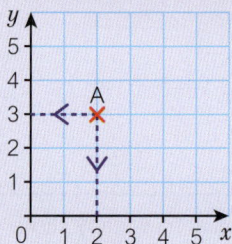

Move down from A (with your finger or a ruler) to the x-axis to find the x-coordinate.
Move across from A (with your finger or a ruler) to the y-axis to find the y-coordinate.

A (2, 3) —— Write the x-coordinate first, then a comma, then the y-coordinate.

2 Copy and complete the coordinates of points A, B, C, D and E.

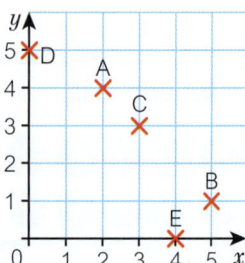

A (2, ☐)   B (☐, 1)

C (3, ☐)   D (☐, 5)

E (☐, ☐)

Midpoints of a line segment

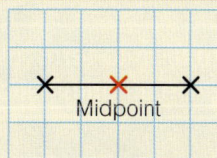

Midpoint

1 Copy this grid.

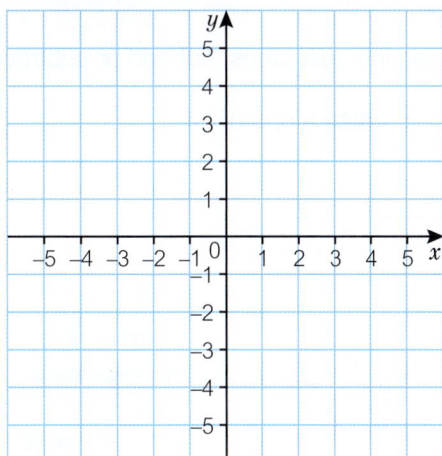

a Plot coordinates A (2, 1) and B (4, 1).

b Use a ruler to draw a line connecting points A and B.

c How many squares is the length of line AB?

d How many squares is half of line AB?

e Place a cross at the midpoint from point A to point B. Write the coordinates of the midpoint.

Q1c hint Count the squares from point A to point B.

Q1e hint Count the squares from point A to halfway along line AB.

2 **a** On the grid in **Q1**, plot coordinates C (1, 1) and D (1, 5).

b Use a ruler to draw a line connecting points C and D.

c How many squares is the length of line CD?

d How many squares is half of line CD?

e Place a cross at the midpoint from point C to point D. Write the coordinates of the midpoint.

Reflect   Write the coordinates of a point in the

a 1st quadrant

b 2nd quadrant

c 3rd quadrant

d 4th quadrant

e Without plotting the point, how do you know that the point (−3, −4) is in the 3rd quadrant?

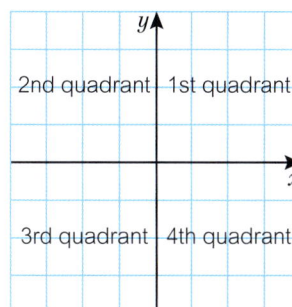

2nd quadrant | 1st quadrant

3rd quadrant | 4th quadrant

9.4 Extending sequences

- Use the term-to-term rule to work out more terms in a sequence
- Recognise an arithmetic sequence and a geometric sequence

Arithmetic sequences

Key point An **arithmetic sequence** goes up or down in equal steps that add or subtract.

For example, the sequence $\overset{+1 \quad +1 \quad +1}{\frown\frown\frown}$ 3, 4, 5, 6, ... goes up in equal steps of +1.

The sequence $\overset{-2 \quad -2 \quad -2}{\frown\frown\frown}$ 10, 8, 6, 4, ... goes down in equal steps of –2.

Guided

1 Which of these are arithmetic sequences?

a $\overset{+2 \quad +2 \quad +2}{\frown\frown\frown}$ 1, 3, 5, 7, ...

b $\overset{-3 \quad -3 \quad -3}{\frown\frown\frown}$ 12, 9, 6, 3, ...

c $\overset{+1 \quad +2 \quad +3}{\frown\frown\frown}$ 1, 2, 4, 7, ...

d $\overset{-1 \quad -2 \quad -3}{\frown\frown\frown}$ 10, 9, 7, 4, ...

Q1 hint Does the sequence go up or down in equal steps that add or subtract? If yes, it is arithmetic. If no, it is not arithmetic.

Key point You can describe an arithmetic sequence using the first term and the **term-to-term rule**.

In an arithmetic sequence the term-to-term rule is also called the **common difference**.

For example, look at this sequence.

$\overset{-4 \quad -4 \quad -4}{\frown\frown\frown}$ 16, 12, 8, 4, ... The common difference is –4.

The first term is 16.

2 Write the first term of each of these arithmetic sequences.

a 9, 11, 13, 15, ...   b 20, 18, 16, 14, ...   c 4, 7, 10, 13, ...   d 2, 12, 22, 32, ...

3 For each sequence, write the first term and the common difference.

a $\overset{+\square \quad +\square \quad +\square}{\frown\frown\frown}$ 5, 9, 13, 17, ...

b $\overset{+\square \quad +\square \quad +\square}{\frown\frown\frown}$ 2, 7, 12, 17, ...

c $\overset{-\square \quad -\square \quad -\square}{\frown\frown\frown}$ 35, 25, 15, 5, ...

d $\overset{-\square \quad -\square \quad -\square}{\frown\frown\frown}$ 20, 17, 14, 11, ...

3 Copy the coordinate grid in **Q2**.
   Plot these coordinates.

   A (3, 5)   B (2, 4)   C (2, 5)
   D (0, 1)   E (5, 3)

Q3 hint For A, point to 3 on the x-axis. Move your finger up until you are level with 5 on the y-axis. Draw a cross. Label it A.

4 **Reasoning**   The coordinates for points A and E in **Q3** use numbers 3 and 5.
   Write a sentence explaining why A and E are not in the same place.

5 Write the values on these number lines.

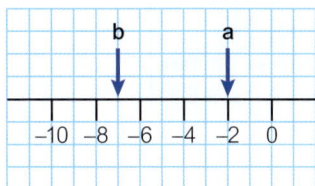

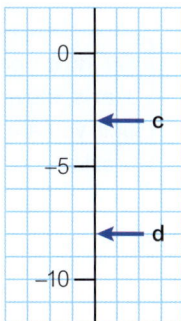

Key point   A coordinate grid can be split into four **quadrants**
(quarters).
The x-coordinate is a value on the x-axis and can be positive
or negative.
The y-coordinate is a value on the y-axis and can be positive
or negative.

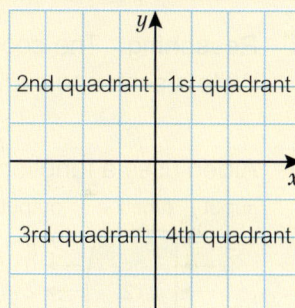

6 Copy and complete the coordinates of points A, B, C, D, E and F.
   The first one has been done for you.

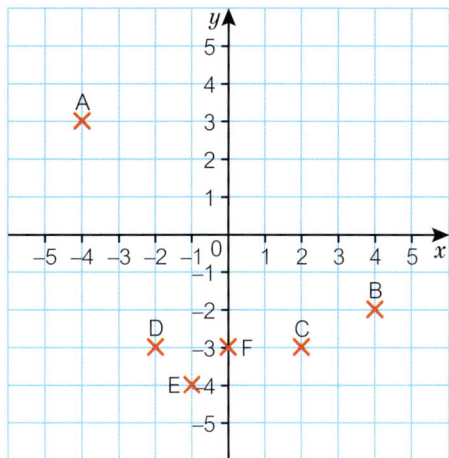

Q6 hint Move up from B with your finger or a ruler to the x-axis to find the x-coordinate.
Move across from C with your finger or a ruler to the y-axis to find the y-coordinate.

   A (−4, 3)   B (□, −2)   C (2, □)
   D (□, −3)   E (□, □)   F (□, □)

Guided

7 Plot these coordinates on the grid. The first one has been done for you.

A (–2, 3)
B (4, –1)
C (–3, –2)
D (1, 4)
E (–4, 1)

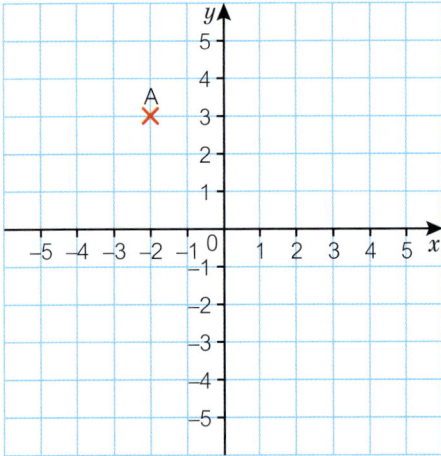

Q7 hint For B, point to 4 on the x-axis. Move your finger down until you are level with –1 on the y-axis. Draw a cross. Label it B.

8 **Reasoning** The coordinates for points B and E in **Q7** use numbers 1, 4, –1, and –4. Write a sentence explaining why B and E are not in the same place.

9 Aiden uses a function machine to help him write some coordinates.

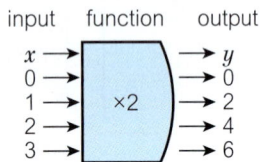

a Write the coordinates from the function machine.
   The first two have been written for you.
   (0, 0)
   (1, 2)
   (☐, ☐)
   (☐, ☐)

b Write the rule that connects x and y.
   $y = ☐☐$

c Aiden writes the coordinates he wants to plot in a table. Copy and complete the table.

x	0	1	2	3	4	5
y	0	2				

Q9b hint Look at the function machine.

Q9c hint Use the rule in **Q9b** to help you complete the table.

Geometric sequences

1   Which of these are geometric sequences?

a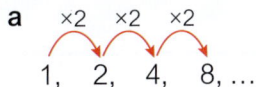
×2   ×2   ×2

1,   2,   4,   8, …

b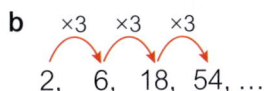
×3   ×3   ×3

2,   6,   18,   54, …

c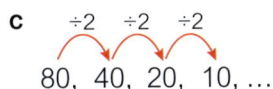
÷2   ÷2   ÷2

80,   40,   20,   10, …

d
×2   ×2   ×2

4,   8,   16,   32, …

e
×2   ×3   ×4

1,   2,   6,   24, …

f
÷3   ÷3   ÷3

27,   9,   3,   1, …

2   The first term and the rule are given for each of these sequences.
Find the next two terms.

a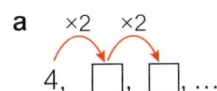
×2   ×2

4, ☐, ☐, …

b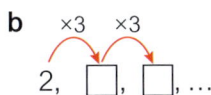
×3   ×3

2, ☐, ☐, …

c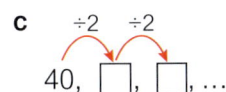
÷2   ÷2

40, ☐, ☐, …

d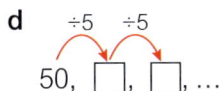
÷5   ÷5

50, ☐, ☐, …

Sequences with two-step rules

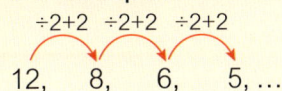

Worked example

A sequence has first term 1.
The term-to-term rule is 'add 3, then multiply by 2'.
Write the first three terms in the sequence.

1st term = 1

2nd term = 1 → (+3) → 4 → (×2) → 8 ——— You can draw a function machine to represent this rule.

3rd term = 8 → (+3) → 11 → (×2) → 22

1, 8, 22

Guided

1 Copy and complete the function machines and write the first three terms in each sequence.

   a First term 3; term-to-term rule is subtract 1, multiply by 2.

   1st term = □

   2nd term = 3 → (−1) → (×2) → □

   3rd term = □ → (−1) → (×2) → □

   b First term 2; term-to-term rule is add 1, multiply by 3.

   1st term = □

   2nd term = 2 → (+1) → (×3) → □

   3rd term = □ → (+1) → (×3) → □

   c First term 7; term-to-term rule is subtract 2, multiply by 2.

   1st term = □

   2nd term = 7 → (−2) → (×2) → □

   3rd term = □ → (□) → (□) → □

   d First term 4; term-to-term rule is add 1, multiply by 2.

   1st term = □

   2nd term = 4 → (□) → (□) → □

   3rd term = □ → (□) → (□) → □

Reflect   The first term of a sequence is 4 and the term-to-term rule is 'add 1, then multiply by 2'.

Draw a function machine and write the first three terms of this sequence.

Joe says that this is the same as a sequence with the term-to-term rule 'multiply by 2, then add 1'.

Show that Joe is incorrect.

9.5 Straight-line graphs

- Recognise, name and plot graphs parallel to the axes
- Recognise, name and plot the graph of $y = x$
- Plot straight-line graphs using a table of values

Graphs parallel to the axes and $y = x$

1 Copy the coordinate grid.

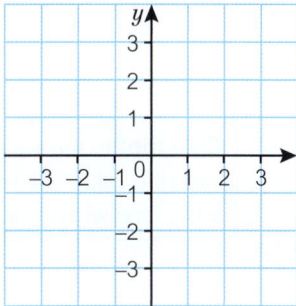

   a Plot these coordinates: (3, 2), (1, 2), (–1, 2), (–3, 2).

   b Use a ruler to join the points with a straight line.

   c Look at the y-coordinate of each point.
     Copy and complete: $y = \square$.

   d Write the coordinates of another point on your straight line.

   e Plot these coordinates: (3, –3), (0, –3), (–3, –3).
     Repeat parts **b**, **c** and **d**.

> **Q1c hint**
> (3,②), (1,②),
> (–1,②), (–3,②)

2 Copy the coordinate grid in **Q1** again.

   a Plot these coordinates: (1, 3), (1, 1), (1, –1), (1, –3).

   b Use a ruler to join these points with a straight line.

   c Look at the x-coordinate of each point.
     Copy and complete: $x = \square$.

   d Write the coordinates of another point on your straight line.

   e Plot these coordinates: (2, 3) (2, 0) (2, –3).
     Repeat parts **b**, **c** and **d**.

> **Q2c hint**
> (①, 3), (①, 1),
> (①, –1), (①, –3)

3 Copy the coordinate grid in **Q1** again.

   a Plot these coordinates: (3, 3), (1, 1), (0, 0), (–3, –3).

   b Use a ruler to join these points with a straight line.

   c Look at the x-coordinate and y-coordinate of each point.
     Copy and complete: $y = \square$.

   d **Problem-solving** Write the coordinates of another point on your straight line.

> **Q3 hint** (③,③)
> has x-coordinate 3
> and y-coordinate 3.
> Now look at (①,①),
> (⓪,⓪), (–③, –③).

Drawing a table of values and plotting straight-line graphs

1 Here is a function machine for $y = x - 1$.

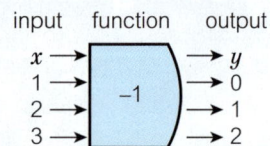

Write the value of y when

a x is 1   **b** x is 2   **c** x is 3

> **Key point**   A function can be used to draw a table of values showing pairs of x- and y-values.
> These x- and y-values can be used as coordinates to plot the graph of the function.

2 a Copy and complete the function machine for $y = x + 5$.

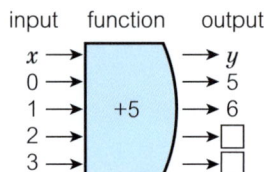

b Use the function machine to copy and complete the table for $y = x + 5$.

x	0	1	2	3
y	5	6		

> **Q2b hint** In the table, write the value of y when x is 2, and when x is 3.

c Copy and complete the pairs of x- and y-values in the table as coordinates.

(0, 5), (1, 6), (2, ☐), (3, ☐)

d Copy the coordinate grid on the right.
Plot the coordinates in **c** on your coordinate grid.
Join the points with a straight line.

e Extend your straight line to the edge of your grid to draw a graph.

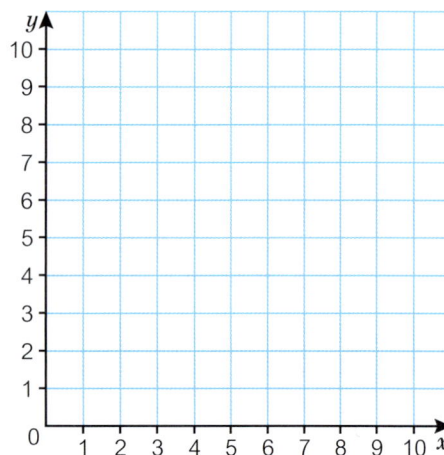

3 a Copy and complete the function machine for $y = 2x$.

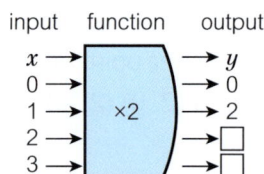

b Use the function machine to copy and complete the table for $y = 2x$.

x	0	1	2	3
y	0	2		

> **Q3d hint** A graph of a function should always go to the edge of the grid.

c Write the pairs of x- and y-values in the table as coordinates.

d Copy the coordinate grid in **Q2** and draw the graph of $y = 2x$.

> **Reflect**   Look back at your graphs.
> How can you tell, by looking at your graph, if you have made a mistake in the table of values?

9.6 Position-to-term rules

- Generate terms of a sequence using a position-to-term rule
- Use linear expressions to describe the nth term of simple sequences

Finding terms of a sequence using the position-to-term rule

Key point Each term in a sequence has a **position**.
The 1st term is in position 1, the 2nd term in position 2, the 3rd term in position 3 and so on.

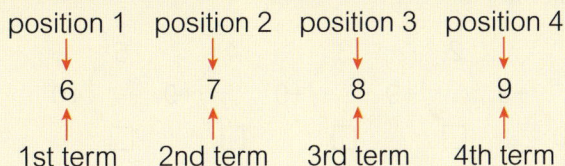

position 1	position 2	position 3	position 4
↓	↓	↓	↓
6	7	8	9
↑	↑	↑	↑
1st term	2nd term	3rd term	4th term

1 Here is a sequence.

position 1
↓
2, 4, 6, 8, 10, ...

The term in position 1 is 2. Write down the term in:

a position 4   **b** position 3   **c** position 2   **d** position 5

Key point This number **sequence** follows two **rules**.

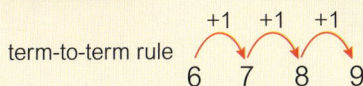

term-to-term rule
+1   +1   +1
6   7   8   9

The **term-to-term rule** is +1

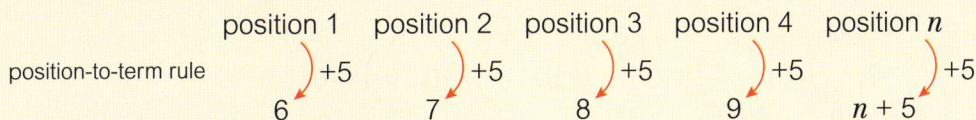

position-to-term rule
position 1   position 2   position 3   position 4   position n
)+5   )+5   )+5   )+5   )+5
6   7   8   9 $n + 5$

The **position-to-term rule** is n +5.

2 Here is a sequence

4, 5, 6, 7, ...

a Copy and complete to find the term-to-term rule.

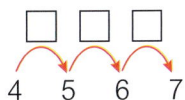

☐ ☐ ☐

4   5   6   7

b Copy and complete to find the position-to-term rule.

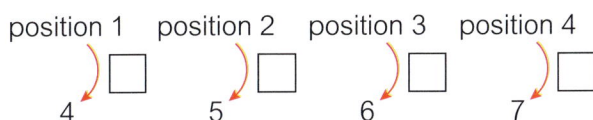

position 1   position 2   position 3   position 4
)☐   )☐   )☐   )☐
4   5   6   7

3 Use the position-to-term rule to copy and complete the first five terms of each sequence. Then copy and complete the position-to-term tables.

a position-to-term rule: $n + 3$

position	1	2	3	4	5
	)+3	)+3	)+3	)+3	)+3
term	4	5	☐	☐	☐

position (n)	1	2	3	4	5
term ($n + 3$)	4	5			

b position-to-term rule: $n + 9$

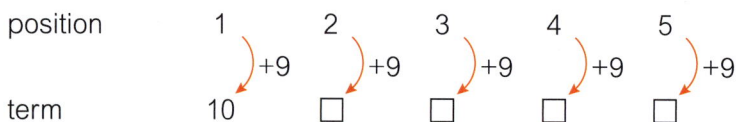

position	1	2	3	4	5
	)+9	)+9	)+9	)+9	)+9
term	10	☐	☐	☐	☐

position (n)	1	2	3	4	5
term ($n + 9$)	10				

c position-to-term rule: $4n$

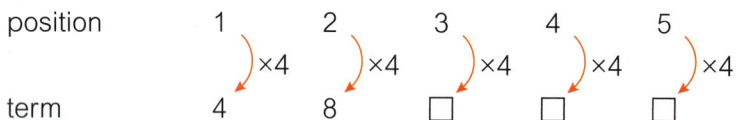

> **Q2c hint** $4n = 4 \times n$

position	1	2	3	4	5
	)×4	)×4	)×4	)×4	)×4
term	4	8	☐	☐	☐

position (n)	1	2	3	4	5
term ($4n$)	4	8			

d position-to-term rule: $10n$

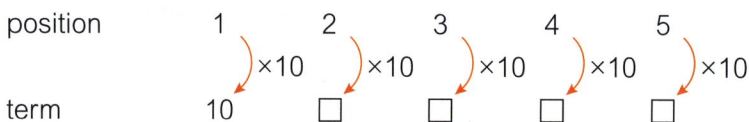

position	1	2	3	4	5
	)×10	)×10	)×10	)×10	)×10
term	10	☐	☐	☐	☐

position (n)	1	2	3	4	5
term ($10n$)	10				

e position-to-term rule: $n - 1$

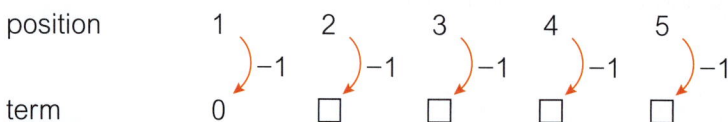

position	1	2	3	4	5
	)−1	)−1	)−1	)−1	)−1
term	0	☐	☐	☐	☐

position (n)	1	2	3	4	5
term ($n - 1$)	0				

Finding the nth term

> **Key point** The position-to-term rule is often referred to as the **nth term**, because it tells you how to work out the term in position n (any position).

1 Copy and complete to find the position-to-term rule for each sequence. The first one has been done for you.

a position   1   2   3

                     +7   +7   +7

     term   8   9   10

b position   1   2   3

                 +☐   +☐   +☐

     term   5   6   7

c position   1   2   3

                 ×☐   ×☐   ×☐

     term   3   6   9

> **Q1c hint** Look carefully at the rule. It is ×☐.

d position   1   2   3

                 ×☐   ×☐   ×☐

     term   8   16   24

2 **Problem-solving** Complete the diagrams in **Q1** by writing the position-to-term rule in terms of n.

> **Q2a hint**
> position   1   2   3 n
>   +7 +7 +7 +7
> term   8   9   10 $n + ☐$

> **Reflect** Write the first five numbers in the 6 times-table. Now you have a sequence.
> Write the position above each number.
> Is the position-to-term rule '×6' or '+6'?
> position   1 ☐ ☐ ☐ ☐
>
> term   6 ☐ ☐ ☐ ☐
>
> What is the term-to-term rule?
>
> 6 ☐ ☐ ☐
>
> Make sure you understand the position-to-term and term-to-term rules.
> Make some notes to help you remember.

10 Transformations

10.1 Congruency and enlargements

- Identify congruent shapes
- Enlarge shapes using given scale factors
- Work out the scale factor given an object and its image

Congruence

Key point   **Congruent** shapes are exactly the same **shape** and **size**.

Guided

1   Choose the shape from the box that is **congruent**. One has been done for you.

> **Q1 hint** Turn your book to see if these shapes look the same shape **and** size.

a

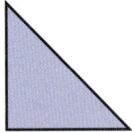

Shape **a** is congruent to shape **iv**

b

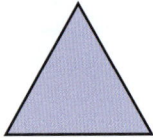

Shape **b** is congruent to shape ☐

c

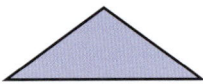

Shape **c** is congruent to shape ☐

d

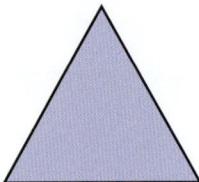

Shape **d** is congruent to shape ☐

i

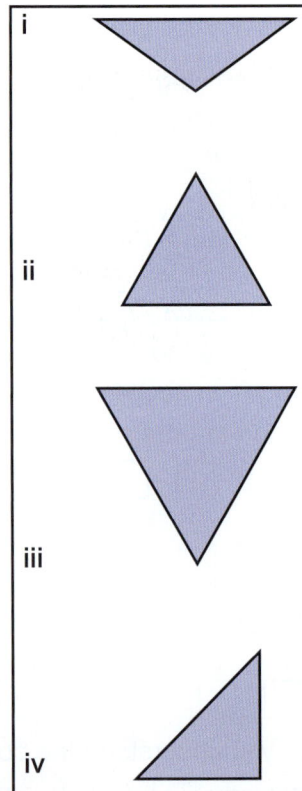

ii

iii

iv

2 Reasoning Are the shapes in each pair congruent? Give a reason for your answer.

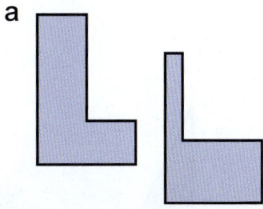

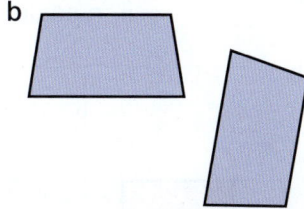

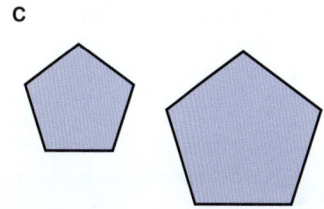

a

b

c

3 Each pair of shapes is congruent.
Find the lengths of the sides marked with letters:

Q3 hint Look for matching sides.

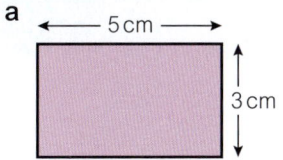

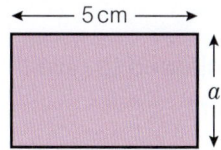

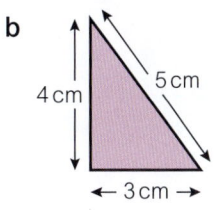

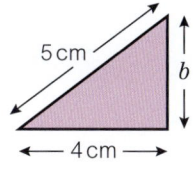

a

← 5 cm →   ← 5 cm →

3 cm a

b

4 cm   5 cm   5 cm b

← 3 cm →   ← 4 cm →

Enlargement

> **Key point**   **Enlargement** is a type of **transformation**. The **scale factor** tells you how much to enlarge the shape by.

Worked example

Enlarge this triangle by a **scale factor** of 2.

Count squares to find the side lengths. Multiply them by the scale factor.

Draw the two enlarged sides. Join them to make the 3rd side.

3

← 2 →

2 × 3 = 6
2 × 2 = 4

6

← 4 →

Guided

1 Copy the diagram onto squared paper.
Enlarge the triangle by a scale factor of 2.
The first line has been drawn for you.

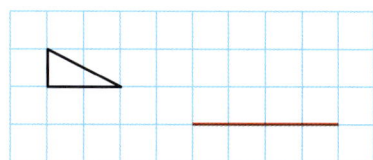

2 Copy these shapes onto squared paper and **enlarge** them by

    i a scale factor of 2   **ii** a scale factor of 3

a   **b** 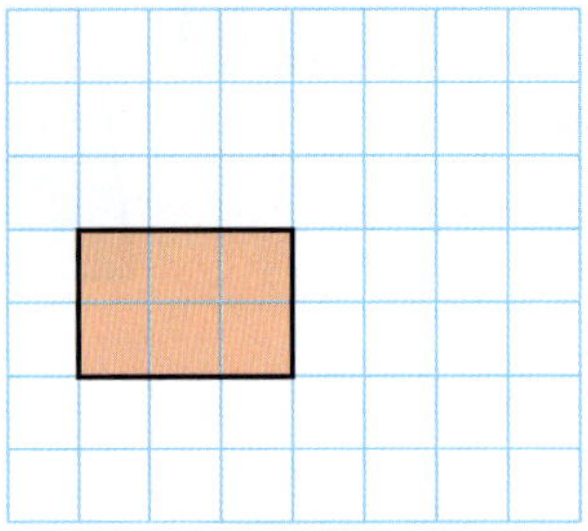   **c**

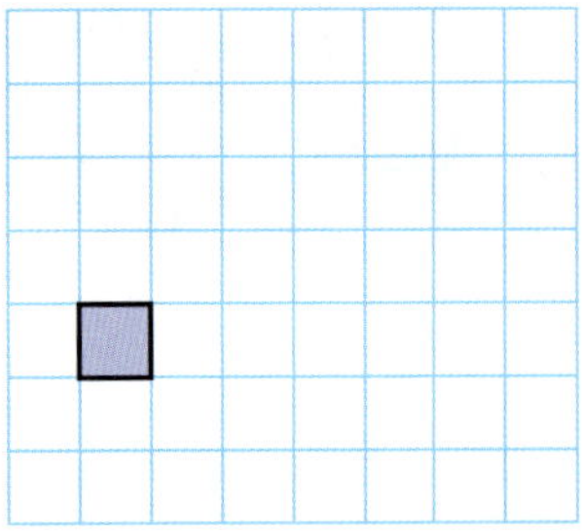

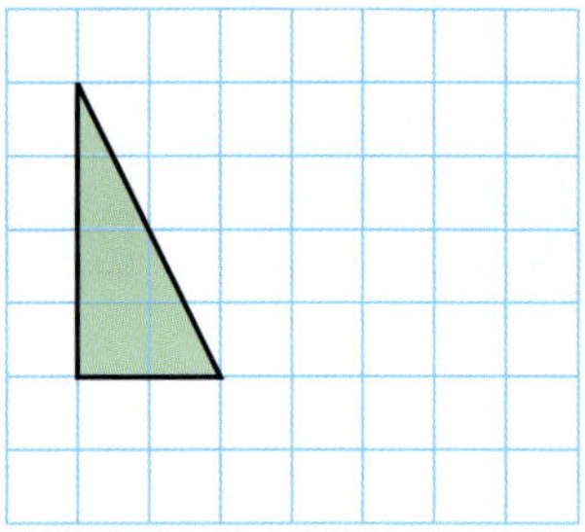

Guided

3 Reasoning   a The original shape is enlarged to give the image.
Write the scale factor of this enlargement.

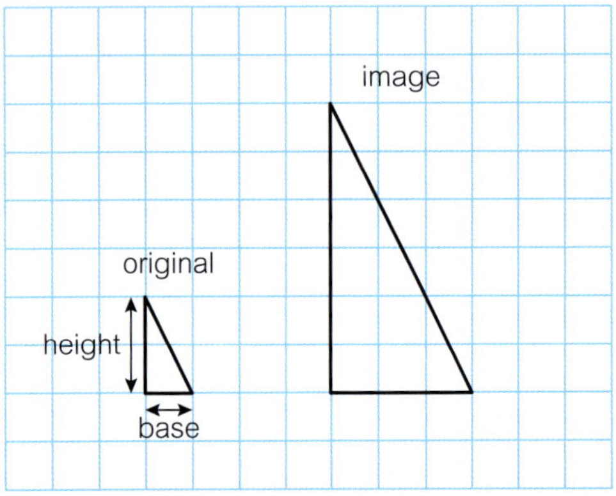

Copy and complete.

Image height = scale factor × original height

          6 = ☐ × 2

Image base = scale factor × original base

          ☐ = ☐ × ☐

Scale factor = ☐

b Find the scale factor of this enlargement.

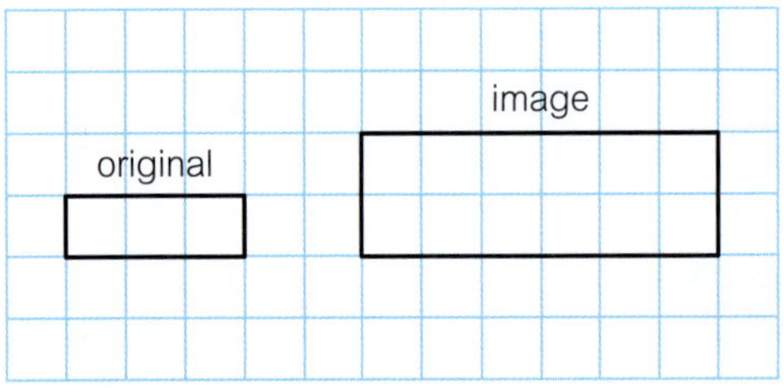

Reflect   Lily writes:

Congruent shapes must be the same shape, the same size and the same way up.

Explain what is wrong with Lily's statement.

10.2 Symmetry

- Recognise line and rotational symmetry in 2D shapes
- Identify all the symmetries of 2D shapes
- Identify reflection symmetry in 3D shapes

Line symmetry

> **Key point** A shape has **line symmetry** if one half folds exactly on top of the other half.
>
>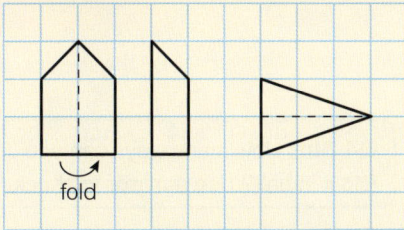
>
> fold
>
> The dashed line is called a **line of symmetry**.

1   Which diagram(s) show a line of symmetry?

a

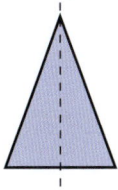

b

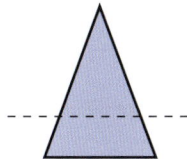

c

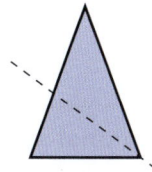

2   State whether each shape has line symmetry or not.

> **Q2 hint** Use a mirror to help you.

a

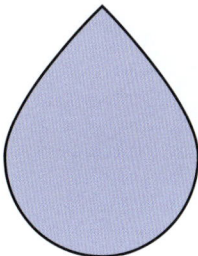

b

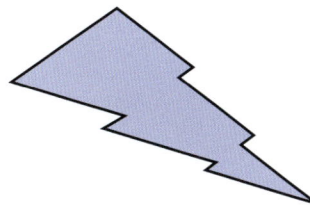

c

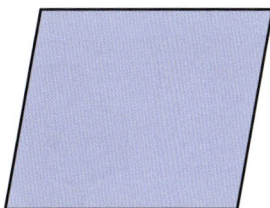

d

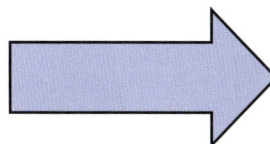

3 Copy each shape onto squared paper. Draw on all the lines of symmetry.

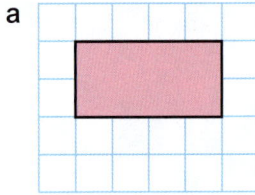

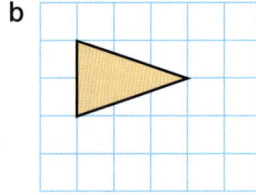

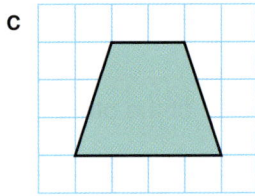

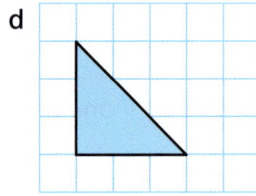

a

b

c

d

4 Write the number of lines of symmetry for each shape.

Q4 hint How many ways can you fold it in half? Use a mirror to check.

Guided

a

b

c

d

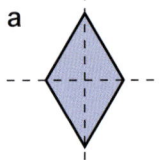

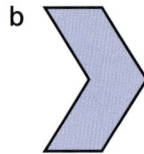

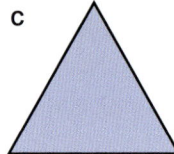

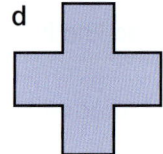

Rotational symmetry

Key point A shape has **rotational symmetry** if it looks the same more than once in a full turn. The number of times the shape looks the same in one rotation is its **order**.

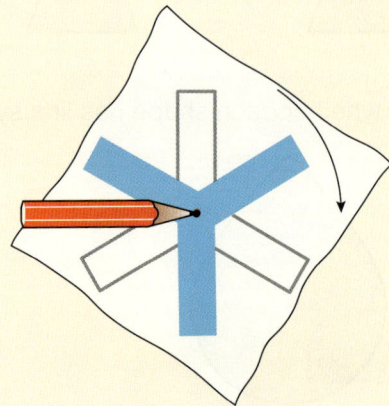

1 Trace each shape. Hold your pencil on the centre dot and rotate your tracing one full turn. How many times does the tracing fit the original shape?

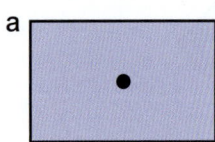

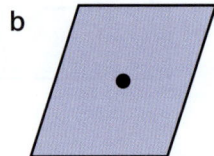

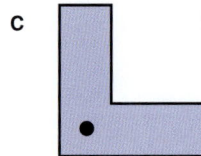

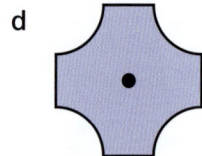

a

b

c

d

2 Find the **order of rotational symmetry** of each shape.

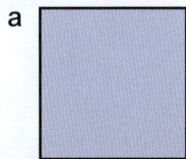

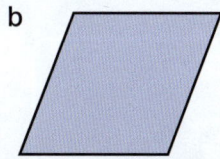

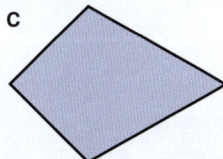

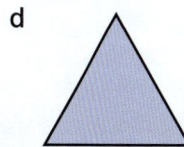

a

b

c

d

Symmetry in 3D shapes

> **Key point** If you can cut a 3D shape into two halves forming mirror images of each other, it has **reflection symmetry**.

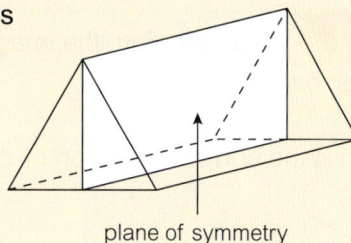

plane of symmetry

1 Copy this cuboid three times.

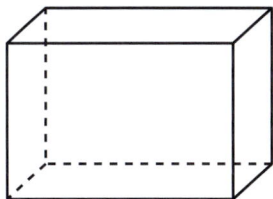

> **Q1a hint** Cut its height in half, its length in half and its width in half.

a Show three different ways that you could cut it so that each half is a mirror image of the other.

b Sketch the plane of symmetry for each one.

2 Which of these objects have reflection symmetry?

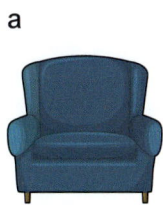

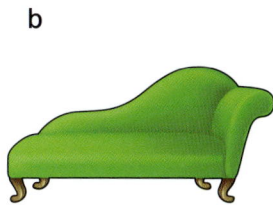

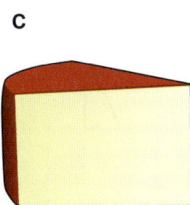

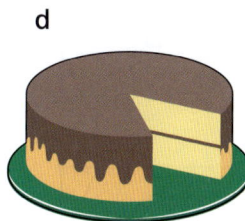

a   b   c   d   e

> **Reflect**   **a**   What objects in the classroom have no lines or planes of symmetry?
> **b**   What objects in the classroom have exactly one line or plane of symmetry?

10.3 Reflection

- Recognise and carry out reflections in a mirror line
- Reflect a shape on a coordinate grid
- Find the mirror line for a reflection on a coordinate grid

Reflections in horizontal and vertical mirror lines

Key point In a reflection, the image is the same size and shape as the original, but 'flipped over'.

1 Which is the correct reflection of the original shape?

Q1 hint You could use a mirror to check.

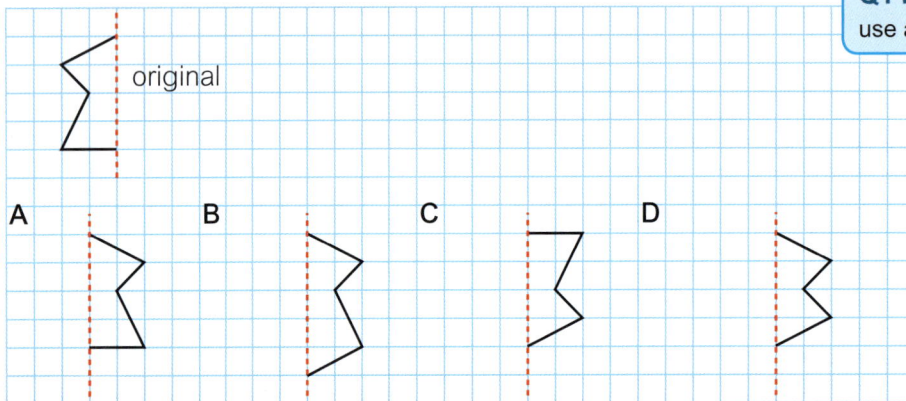

original

A   B   C   D

Key point All points on the **image** are the same distance from the mirror line as the points on the original.

2 Which of **A**, **B** or **C** shows a reflection in the mirror line?

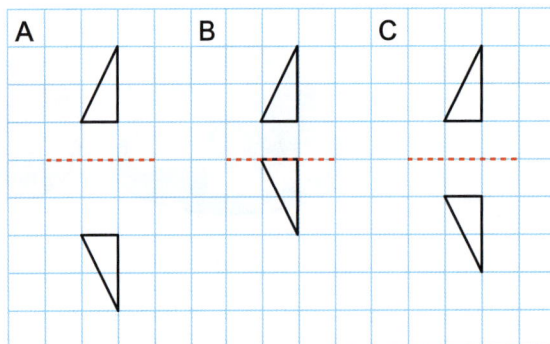

A   B   C

3 Copy and complete each picture to make an accurate reflection in the mirror line.

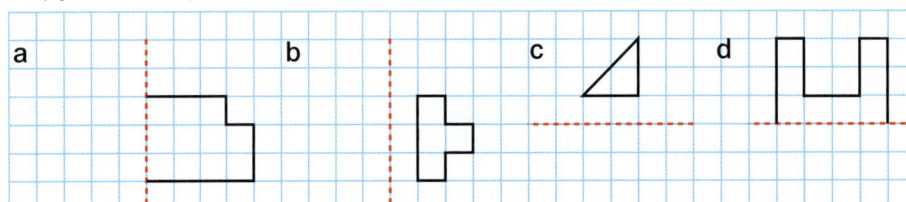

a   b   c   d

135

Reflections on a coordinate grid

1 Copy the coordinate grids. Draw the reflection of each shape
   a in the line $x = 4$ **b** in the line $y = 4$

2 Copy the diagram. Draw in the mirror line for each reflection.

Label each mirror line with its equation.

Reflections in diagonal lines

1 Copy the diagram. Draw the reflection of each shape in the mirror line.

> **Q1 hint** You could turn the page so the mirror line is horizontal or vertical, to help you.

> **Reflect**   Tristan says: 'The mirror line is always halfway between the original and its image.'
> Use examples from this lesson to show he is correct.

10.4　Rotation

* Draw and describe rotations

Describing rotations

1　**a**　Which of these shapes have been rotated 180° ($\frac{1}{2}$ a turn)?

　　i　　　**ii**　　　**iii**　

　　b　Which of these shapes have been rotated 90° ($\frac{1}{4}$ of a turn)?
　　　　Is the rotation clockwise or anticlockwise?

　　i　　　**ii**　　　**iii**　

2　These shapes marked A have been rotated about a centre ✕.
　　Write the rotations that are

> **Q2 hint** Use tracing paper to help you.

　　i　90° clockwise　　**ii**　90° anticlockwise　　**iii**　180°

3　Shape A rotates onto Shape B.

　　a　What is the angle of rotation?

　　b　Is the rotation clockwise or anticlockwise?

　　c　The centre of rotation is on the *x*-axis. Use tracing paper to find its coordinates.

　　d　Use your answers to **a**, **b** and **c** to describe the rotation that takes Shape A onto Shape B.

> **Q3 hint** Rotation ___°, _____, centre (　,0)

Drawing rotations

1   Copy each shape onto squared paper. Rotate it through the angle given about the centre of
rotation marked **×**.

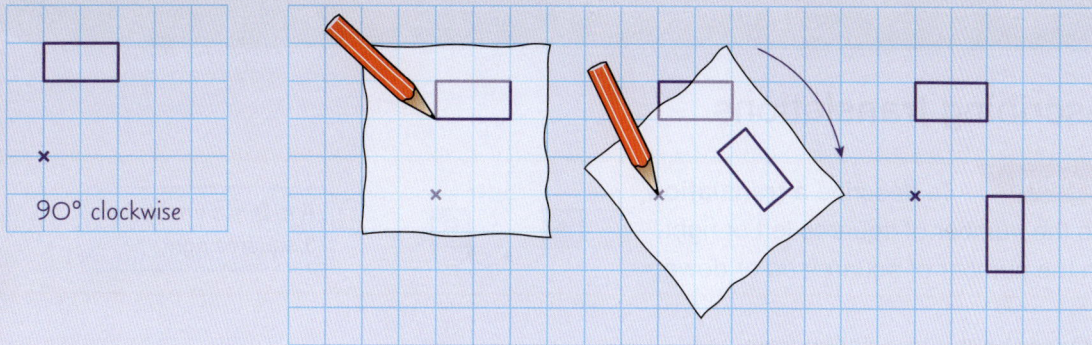

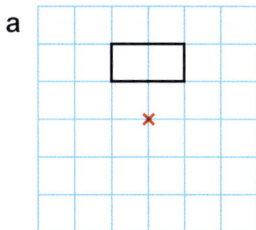

a

180°

b

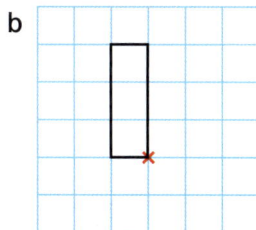

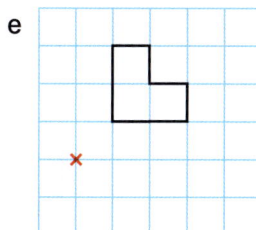

90° anticlockwise

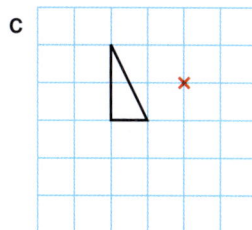

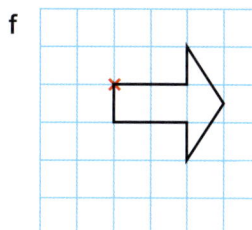

c

270° anticlockwise

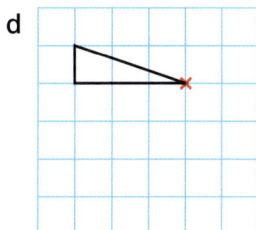

d

180°

e

90° clockwise

f

270° clockwise

Reflect   Use your answers to **Q1** to help you complete these statements with 'vertical' or
'horizontal'.

Rotating a vertical line 90° gives a _____ line

Rotating a horizontal line 180° gives a _____ line

Rotating a _____ line 90° gives a vertical line.

10.5   Translations and combined transformations

- Translate 2D shapes
- Transform 2D shapes by combinations of transformations

Describing translations

Key point To describe a **translation**, write the number of squares left or right, then the number of squares up or down.

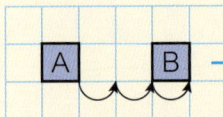

A to B is a translation 3 squares right.

1   Describe the translation from
  a A to B   ☐ squares ____
  b A to C   ☐ squares ____
  c B to C   ☐ squares right and ☐ squares ____

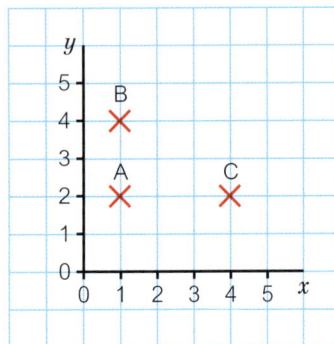

2   Describe each translation.
    The first one has been done for you.
    a A to B   4 squares left
    b A to C
    c A to D
    d A to E
    e B to A
    f C to A
    g D to A
    h E to A

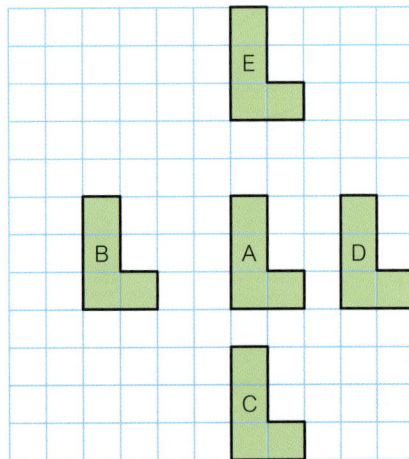

Q2 hint Choose a corner of your first shape and count the squares to the same corner on the second shape.

3   Describe each translation.
    The first one has been done for you.
    a A to B   3 squares right and 1 square down
    b A to C   **c** A to D   **d** A to E
    e B to C   **f** B to D   **g** B to E

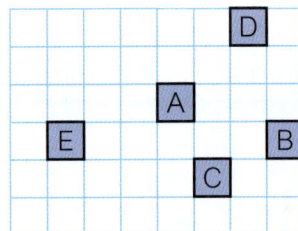

Guided

139

Drawing translations

Guided

1   Copy each shape and **translate** it by the number of squares given.
    The first one has been done for you.

    a 2 squares right   **b** 3 squares down   **c** 4 squares left

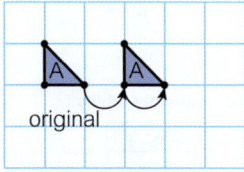

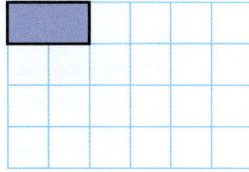

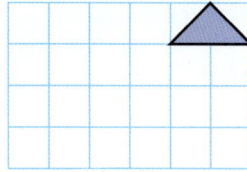

> **Q1 hint** Count the squares from each corner and draw a dot. Then join up the corners.

Worked example

Translate the triangle 5 squares left and 3 squares down.

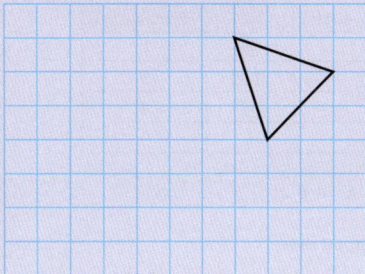

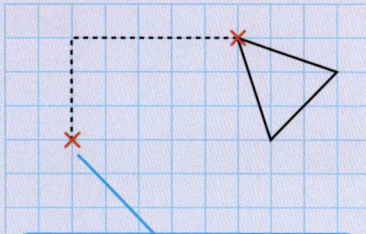

> Choose one of the corners and translate it 5 left, 3 down.

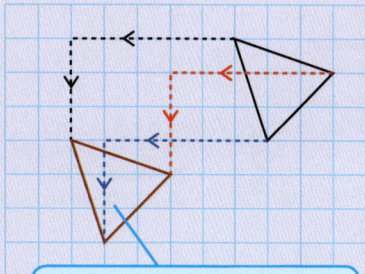

> Repeat for the other corners.

2   Copy each shape onto squared paper. Translate the shapes as follows.

    a 4 squares right, 1 square up   **b** 3 squares left, 2 squares up
    c 2 squares right, 3 squares up   **d** 3 squares left, 2 squares down

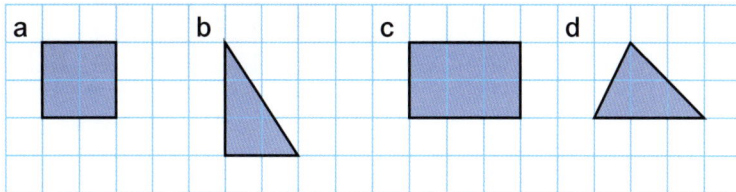

Combined transformations

1   Copy Shape A onto squared paper.

    a Translate Shape A 2 squares right and 3 squares down.
       Label the image B.
    b Translate Shape B 4 squares left and 4 squares up.
       Label the image C.
    c Describe the transformation that takes Shape A **directly** to Shape C.

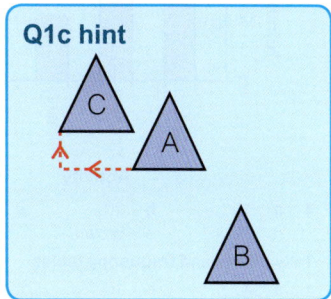

> **Q1c hint**
>

Reflect   **a**   Write down the different types of transformation you have met in this unit.
b   Draw an example to explain each one.

Answers

Unit 1 Analysing and displaying data

1.1 Mode, median and range

Range

1 a 14   b 5   c 14 – 5 = 9
2 a 2, 2, 5, 7, 10
  b Range = 10 – 2 = 8
3 a 5, 10, 12, 13, 20. Range = 15
  b 10, 12, 23, 32. Range = 22
  c 8, 15, 21, 30. Range = 22
4 a 3   b 12   c 9

Mode

1 green
2 blue
3 12
4 a 4   b 14
5 a win   b 4

Median

1 a 6 cm   b 3 cm
2 a, b 10 cm
3 a 3, 4, 5, 6, 7. Median = 5
  b 7, 8, 9, 12, 14, 16, 18. Median = 12
  c 11, 12, 14, 19, 20. Median = 14
  d 10, 20, 30, 30, 40, 50, 60. Median = 30
4 4
5 a 6   b 9

1.2 Displaying data

Pictograms

1 a 3
  b The fruit Mark ate most was pear.
  c 1
2 a 4   b 1   c 3
3 a 2   b 8   c 1   d red

Bar charts

1 a 1   b 2   c 5
  d 20   e 10
2 a 2 students chose swimming.
  b cinema
  c i 5   ii 6   iii 1
3

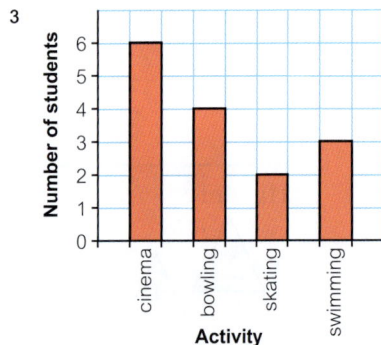

4 a 10   b 20   c 10
  d 70   e brown

Tally charts and frequency tables

1 a 4   b 10   c 12
2 a ||| b 𝍩𝍩 || c 𝍩𝍩 𝍩𝍩 ||||
3 a 4   b 18   c 𝍩𝍩 𝍩𝍩 𝍩𝍩 𝍩𝍩 |
  d bus

4 a

Big cat	Tally	Frequency
lion	𝍩𝍩 𝍩𝍩 ||||	12
tiger	𝍩𝍩 ||	7
cheetah	|||	3
leopard	𝍩𝍩		6
jaguar	𝍩𝍩	5

  b 5   c tiger   d lion
5 a 10   b 25   c 5

1.3 Grouping data

Grouped tally charts and frequency tables

1

Group	Tally	Frequency
1–3	||||	4
4–6	||||	4
7–9	||	2
10–12	||||	4

2 a

Number of books	Tally	Frequency
1–3	𝍩𝍩	5
4–6	𝍩𝍩 ||||	9
7–9	||||	4
10–12			1

  b i 1–3   ii 4–6
  c 4–6

Bar charts for grouped data

1 a 5, 6, 7, 8, 9   b 3   c 15–19
2 a 5   b 14
3 a 5–9
  b

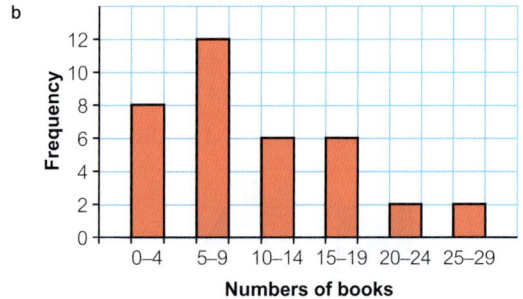

4 a 4   b 6   c 20

1.4 Averages and comparing data

Mean

1 a 6 ÷ 2 = 3
  b (7 + 5 + 9) ÷ 3 = 21 ÷ 3 = 7
  c (4 + 6 + 5 + 1) ÷ 4 = 16 ÷ 4 = 4
  d (1 + 2 + 2 + 2 + 3) ÷ 5 = 10 ÷ 5 = 2
2 a 19   b 5   c 3.8
3 a 44   b 11   c 11
4 a £5.00   b £2.50   c £2.50

Comparing sets of data

1 a 152 cm   b 146 cm   c 146 cm   d 14 cm
2 a smaller than
  b larger than
  c more spread
3 a Club A: $\frac{24}{8}$ = 3; Club B: $\frac{24}{8}$ = 3
  b Club A: 2; Club B: 5
  c

	Mean	Range
Club A	3	2
Club B	3	5

  d i the same as   ii smaller than, less spread

1.5 Line graphs and more bar charts

Line graphs

1 a 40 **b** 8 am **c** decrease **d** increase

2

Number of emails Marcus received

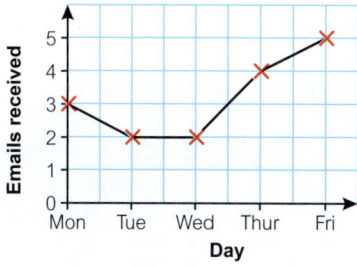

Dual bar charts

1 a

Travelling method to school

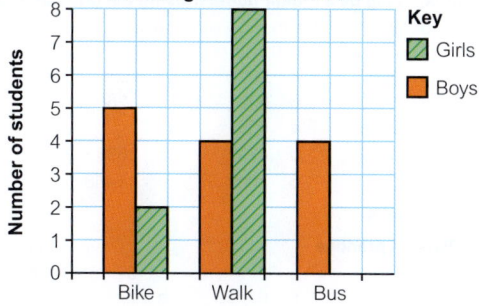

b Because no girls travel by bus.

2 a 3 **b** black

c Because no boys have white phone covers.

d 4 **e** blue **f** 30

Compound bar charts

1 a 20 **b** 30 **c** 60

2 a 20

b

Visitors to a park

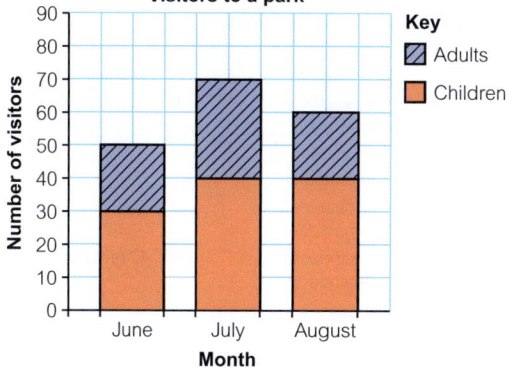

c August

Unit 2 Number skills

2.1 Mental maths

Times tables practice

1 a 6   b 12   c 48   d 63
2 a 3   b 4   c 8   d 11
   e 7   f 5   g 21   h 40
3 a 30   b 36   c 72

Multiplying and dividing by 10, 100 and 1000

1 a 50   b 500   c 5000   d 20
   e 900   f 24 000
2 a 700   b 70   c 7
   d 24   e 13   f 19
3 a 2   b 3   c 4   d 6

Priority of operations

1 a $4 + 10 = 14$
   b 34   c 29   d 29
2 a $10 - 6 = 4$
   b 24   c 18   d 7
3 a $8 + 10 = 18$
   b 13   c 14   d 11
4 a $14 - 4 = 10$
   b 1   c 4   d 1
5 a 9   b 9   c 3   d 3
   e 9   f 9   g 24   h 24
6 a 10   b 11   c 14   d 11
   e 16   f 2   g 1   h 10

2.2 Addition and subtraction

Rounding to the nearest 10, 100 and 1000

1 a i 50   ii 40
   b i 100   ii 200
   c i 7000   ii 8000
2 a 70   b 500   c 2000   d 6000

Addition

1 a

$$
\begin{array}{c}
17 \quad + \quad 22 \\
10 + 7 \quad + \quad 20 + 2 \\
\boxed{10} + \boxed{20} \quad + \quad \boxed{7} + \boxed{2} \\
\boxed{30} \quad + \quad \boxed{9} \\
\boxed{39}
\end{array}
$$

b

$$
\begin{array}{c}
32 \quad + \quad 43 \\
30 + 2 \quad + \quad \boxed{40} + \boxed{3} \\
\boxed{30} + \boxed{40} \quad + \quad \boxed{2} + \boxed{3} \\
\boxed{70} \quad + \quad \boxed{5} \\
\boxed{75}
\end{array}
$$

c

$$
\begin{array}{c}
37 \quad + \quad 33 \\
\boxed{30} + \boxed{7} \quad + \quad \boxed{30} + \boxed{3} \\
\boxed{30} + \boxed{30} \quad + \quad \boxed{7} + \boxed{3} \\
\boxed{60} \quad + \quad \boxed{10} \\
\boxed{70}
\end{array}
$$

d

$$
\begin{array}{c}
69 \quad + \quad 75 \\
\boxed{60} + \boxed{9} \quad + \quad \boxed{70} + \boxed{5} \\
\boxed{60} + \boxed{70} \quad + \quad \boxed{9} + \boxed{5} \\
\boxed{130} \quad + \quad \boxed{14} \\
\boxed{144}
\end{array}
$$

e

$$
\begin{array}{c}
19 \quad + \quad 78 \\
\boxed{10} + \boxed{9} \quad + \quad \boxed{70} + \boxed{8} \\
\boxed{10} + \boxed{70} \quad + \quad \boxed{9} + \boxed{8} \\
\boxed{80} \quad + \quad \boxed{17} \\
\boxed{97}
\end{array}
$$

2 a 74   b 22   c 97   d 61
   e 6
3 a 98   b 93   c 159
4 a i 1   ii 363
   b i 1 ten and 5 ones   ii 465
5 a 828
   b 1386

Subtraction

1 a 54   b 44   c 43   d 37
   e 17   f 69
2 a 12   b 61   c 53   d 111
   e 111   f 211   g 424   h 215
3 a 46   b 16   c 28   d 17

2.3 Multiplication

Multiplying by a single digit using the grid method

1 a $5 \times 70 = 5 \times 7 \times 10 = 35 \times 10 = 350$
   b $6 \times 70 = 6 \times 7 \times 10 = 42 \times 10 = 420$
   c $80 \times 4 = 8 \times 4 \times 10 = 32 \times 10 = 320$
   d $5 \times 600 = 5 \times 6 \times 100 = 30 \times 100 = 3000$
   e $4 \times 7000 = 4 \times 7 \times 1000 = 28 \times 1000 = 28\,000$
2 a 371   b 504   c 455
3 a 1032   b 924   c 2630
4 a 126

Multiplying by a 2-digit number using the grid method

1 a $2 \times 4 \times 10 \times 10 = 8 \times 100 = 800$
   b $4 \times 6 \times 10 \times 10 = 24 \times 100 = 2400$
   c 2000   d 6000
2 a 2666   b 837   c 4368
   d 2448   e 6391
3 a 1612   b 3792   c 1536
4 a 2409   b 7602   c 11 456

2.4 Division

Division practice

1 a 9   b 6   c 6   d 9
   e 9   f 6   g 7   h 5
   i 7
2 a 3   b 4   c 2   d 9

Short division without remainders

1 a 62   b 312   c 121   d 213
2 a 231   b 122   c 322
3 a 181   b 192   c 252
4 a 73   b 91   c 81
5 a 102   b 107   c 206

Short division with remainders

1 a 2   b 1   c 2
   d 6 remainder 1   e 4 remainder 2
2 a 21 remainder 2   b 32 remainder 1
   c 21 remainder 1
3 a 26 remainder 1   b 24 remainder 2
   c 14 remainder 3
4 a 221 remainder 1   b 212 remainder 3
   c 113 remainder 1
5 a 27 remainder 2   b 42 remainder 1
   c 48 remainder 2

2.5 Time and money

Working with money

1 a £0.50   b £0.05   c £0.20
   d £0.02   e £0.07   f £0.70
   g £0.03   h £0.30
2 £0.95 = 95p   £0.55 = 55p   £5.05 = 505p
   £1.50 = 150p   £1.05 = 105p   £9.50 = 950p
3 a

   b A : £7   B : £7   C : £7
4 a £3   b £3   c £3   d £3
   e £4   f £4   g £4   h £4
5 a £8   b £5   c £7   d £15

Working with time

1 a 60   b 120   c 180   d 600
2 a 130 minutes   b 345 minutes
   c 258 minutes

3 a 2 hours and 30 minutes
  b 3 hours and 20 minutes
  c 5 hours and 12 minutes

4 a $\frac{1}{2}$ hour = $\frac{1}{2} \times 60$ = 30 minutes

  b $\frac{1}{4}$ hour = $\frac{1}{4} \times 60$ = 15 minutes

  c $\frac{3}{4}$ hour = $\frac{3}{4} \times 60$ = 45 minutes

  d 0.1 hour = 0.1 × 60 = 6 minutes
  e 0.6 hour = 0.6 × 60 = 36 minutes
  f 0.25 hour = 0.25 × 60 = 15 minutes
  g 0.5 hour = 0.5 × 6 = 30 minutes
  h 0.75 hour = 0.75 × 60 = 45 minutes

5 a T   b F   c F   d F
  e T   f F

2.6 Negative numbers

Ordering positive and negative numbers

1 3, 11, 19, 45, 64, 71, 123
2 a A = 7 °C, B = 1 °C, C = –2 °C. D = –6 °C, E = –9 °C
  b A   c E
3 a, b i 1 °C < <u>7 °C</u>
       ii <u>1 °C</u> > –6 °C
       iii <u>–2 °C</u> > –6 °C
       iv –9 °C < <u>–2 °C</u>
4 a i Iceland   ii England
  b –20, –5, 3
5 a –5, –3, 4
  b –3, –1, 1, 2
  c –8, –5, 4, 6, 10
  d –9, –8, –4, –2, 1
6 a 6   b 4   c 3   d 1
  e 0
7 a 4   b 5   c 6   d 5
  e 6   f 7   g –6   h –4
  i 0   j –8   k –5   l 1

Subtraction calculations that give negative numbers

1 a –2   b –3   c –4   d –4
  e –6   f –8   g –1   h –4
  i –6   j –4   k –6   l –9
2 a –4   b –5   c –6   d –8
  e –6

2.7 Factors, multiples and primes

Multiples

1 a 3, 6, 9, 12, 15
  b 4, 8, 12, 16, 20
  c 6, 12, 18, 24, 30
  d 8, 16, 24, 32, 40
2 a 2, 4, 6, 8, 10, 12, 14, 16, 18
  b 5, 10, 15
  c 10
3 a 3, 6, 9, 12, 15, 18, 21, 24
  b 5, 10, 15
  c 15
4 a 30   b 20   c 60
5 a

Number	First 10 multiples
5	5, 10, 15, 20, 25, 30, 35, 40, 45, 50
6	6, 12, 18, 24, 30, 36, 42, 48, 54, 60
7	7, 14, 21, 28, 35, 42, 49, 56, 63, 70
8	8, 16, 24, 32, 40, 48, 56, 64, 72, 80

  b i 30   ii 35   iii 40
    iv 42   v 24   vi 56

Factors

1 a Yes, 1 × 12 = 12
  b Yes, 2 × 6 = 12
  c Yes, 3 × 4 = 12
  d No
  e No
  f 1, 2, 3, 4, 6, 12

2 a 1, 3, 5, 15
  b 1, 2, 3, 6, 9, 18
  c 1, 5, 25
  d 1, 2, 3, 4, 6, 8, 12, 24
3 a 15: 1, 3, 5, 15   25: 1, 5, 25
  b 1, 5   c 5
4 a

Number	Factors
16	1, 2, 4, 8, 16
20	1, 2, 4, 5, 10, 20
24	1, 2, 3, 4, 6, 8, 12, 24
28	1, 2, 4, 7, 14, 28
30	1, 2, 3, 5, 6, 10, 15, 30

  b i 4   ii 8   iii 4
    iv 2   v 4   vi 4
    vii 10   viii 4

Primes

1 a

Number	Factors	Number of factors
1	1	1
2	1, 2	2
3	1, 3	2
4	1, 2, 4	3
5	1, 5	2
6	1, 2, 3, 6	4
7	1, 7	2
8	1, 2, 4, 8	4
9	1, 3, 9	3
10	1, 2, 5, 10	4
11	1, 11	2
12	1, 2, 3, 4, 6, 12	6

  b 2, 3, 5, 7, 11
  c 2, 3, 5, 7, 11

2.8 Square numbers

Recognising square numbers

1 a A and C   b 9 and 16
2 a $2^2 = 2 \times 2 = 4$
    $3^2 = 3 \times 3 = 9$
    $4^2 = 4 \times 4 = 16$
    $5^2 = 5 \times 5 = 25$
  b $6^2 = 6 \times 6 = 36$
    $7^2 = 7 \times 7 = 49$
    $8^2 = 8 \times 8 = 64$
    $9^2 = 9 \times 9 = 81$
  c 9
3 a 324   b 625   c 8281
  d 11 664   e 45 369
4 Squaring is multiplying a number by itself, not by 2.
   For example, squaring 4 is 4 × 4 = 16.

Square roots

1 a 4 rows, 4 columns
  b 5 rows, 5 columns
2 a 2   b 6   c 10
3 a 1   b 3   c 5
  d 7   e 11
4 a 20   b 13   c 18   d 25

Powers in priority of operations

1 a 11   b 25, 29   c 9, 4
  d 16, 32   e 36, 18   f 4, 6

Unit 3 Expressions, functions and formulae

3.1 Functions

One-step function machines

1 a 9   b 4   c 20   d 8
2 a 24   b 3   c 13   d 7
3 a $2 + 5 = 7, 3 + 5 = 8, 4 + 5 = 9$
   b 5, 8, 11
4 a 3, 9, 18   b 4, 5, 10
5 a $+3$ b $\times 2$
6 a $+5, \times 2$ b $+5$

Two-step function machines

1 a $3 \times 2 = 6, 6 - 3 = 3$
     $5 \times 2 = 10, 10 - 3 = 7$
     $9 \times 2 = 18, 18 - 3 = 15$
   b $10 \div 5 = 2, 2 + 4 = 6$
     $15 \div 5 = 3, 3 + 4 = 7$
     $25 \div 5 = 5, 5 + 4 = 9$

3.2 Simplifying expressions 1

Simplifying expressions by adding or subtracting like terms

1 a $x + x = 2x$ b $3x$ c $3x$
   d $4x$ e $4x$ f $5x$
2 a $2m$ b $3m$ c $7m$ d $9m$
3 a $3y$ b $4y$ c $2y$
4 Ena is correct. $3x - x$ is the same as $3x - 1x = 2x$.

Simplifying expressions by adding and subtracting like terms

1 a $5m$ b $3m$ c $5m$ d $5x$

Simplifying expressions involving variables and numbers

1 $2x, 5x, x; y, 2y, 6y; m, 4m$
2 a $7x$ b $7x + 2$ c $7x + y$ d $7x + 3y$
   e $5y$ f $3x$ g $8p$
3 a $x + y + 2x = x + 2x + y$
   b $2x + 3x + 2y$ c $3p + p + 5t$
   d $4m - 3m + 2n$
4 a $4x + 2y - 2x = 4x - 2x + 2y = 2x + 2y$
   b $3x + 3y$ c $p + 4t$ d $3m + 3n$

3.3 Simplifying expressions 2

Multiply algebraic terms

1 a $4y$ b $7t$ c $6a$ d $10f$
2 a pq b mn c ab
3 a $6b$ b $12y$ c $10p$
   d $8b$ e $18a$ f $18a$
4 a $4x$ b $2x$ c $5x$

Working with brackets

1 a $3 \times (20 + 7) = 3 \times 20 + 3 \times 7 = 60 + 21 = 81$
   b $4 \times (30 + 2) = 4 \times 30 + 4 \times 2 = 120 + 8 = 128$
2 a $5 \times 20 + 5 \times 3 = 100 + 15 = 115$
   b $4 \times 50 + 4 \times 3 = 200 + 12 = 212$
   c $3 \times 20 + 3 \times 6 = 60 + 18 = 78$
3 a $2 \times (30 - 3) = 60 - 6 = 54$
   b $80 - 12 = 68$
4 a $240 - 4 = 236$
   b $3(60 - 2) = 180 - 6 = 174$
   c $2(80 - 2) = 160 - 4 = 156$
5 a $4a + 20$ b $3a - 6$

3.4 Writing expressions

Writing expressions from word descriptions

1 a $n + 4$ b $n - 2$ c $3n$
2 a $c + 5$ b $c - 3$ c $7c$
3 a $a + 4$ b $a + 10$ c $a - 6$
   d $a - 4$ e $2a$
4 a $x + 4$ b $3x$ c $6x$

Write expressions using function machines

1 a i $y + 5$ ii 16
   b i $m - 6$ ii 9
   c i $5p$ ii 15
   d i $\frac{z}{4}$ ii 2
2 a B   b A   c D   d C
3 a C   b A   c B   d D

3.5 Substituting into formulae

Formulae written in words

1 a 10 cm   b 15 cm   c 20 cm   d 50 cm
2 a 40 km   b 50 km   c 60 km   d 100 km
3 a 24   b 32   c 40   d 80

Formulae written in letters

1 a $T = 8 + 5 = 13$
   b $T = 8 + 10 = 18$ c $T = 8 + 15 = 23$
2 a $h = 10, W = 15 \times 10 = 150$
   b 450   c 525
3 a Area = length × width = $2 \times 5 = 10\,\text{cm}^2$
   b $60\,\text{cm}^2$ c $12\,\text{cm}^2$
4 a 30 cm   b 20 cm   c 40 cm
5 a L = length, P = perimeter
   b i 10 cm   ii 5 cm   iii 4 cm

3.6 Writing formulae

Using function machines to write formulae in words and letters

1 a

   b number of balls = number of students + 4 balls
   c $b = s + 4$
2 a

   b number of mats = number of students – 2 mats
   c $m = s - 2$

Using patterns to write formulae in words and letters

1 a total cost = 2 × £2
   b total cost = 3 × £2
   c $c = p \times 2 = 2p$
2 a i number of cheese slices = 5×2
     ii number of cheese slices = 10×2
     iii $n = 2 \times b = 2b$
   b i When $b = 2$ $n = 2 \times 2 = 4$
     ii When $b = 3$ $n = 2 \times 3 = 6$

Unit 4 Decimals and measures

4.1 Decimals and rounding

Understanding decimals with tenths

1 a Yes   b No   c Yes   d Yes
2 a 2.1, 2.5   b 2.5, 7.5
3 a 0.5   b 0.7   c 1.2
4 a 4.3 cm   b 0.9 cm   c 8.4 cm   d 11.1 cm
5 a 5 cm   b 6.8 cm   c 3.5 cm
6 Student's own answers
7 23.9, 1.7, 3.0, 8.8

Understanding decimals with tenths and hundredths

1 a 0.06   b 0.74   c 1.35
2 a

T	O	·	t	h
i		3		
ii		3		1
iii		3		0	6

   b i 1   ii 6
3 a i zero point four   ii 4 tenths
   b i zero point seven four   ii 4 hundredths
   c i zero point zero four   ii 4 hundredths
   d i one point four one   ii 4 tenths

Ordering decimals

1 a 2 tenths   b 8 tenths
   c zero tenths   d zero tenths
2 a 0.4   b 0.8   c 0.73   d 0.7
3 a $1.2 < 1.5$ b $2.4 > 1.5$
   c $7.1 > 7.08$ d $1.14 < 1.2$
4 a any decimal greater than .4
   b any decimal less than .1
   c any decimal greater than 8.7
   d repeat parts a to c with a suitable different answer
5 a 1.1, 1.2, 1.3, 1.4, 1.7
   b 2.31, 2.32, 2.34, 2.35, 2.39
   c 8.03, 8.12, 8.3, 8.31, 8.4
   d 7.01, 7.04, 7.09, 7.1, 7.11

Rounding decimals

1 a 3 cm   b 5 cm   c 6 cm
2 a A = 0.8, B = 2.1, C = 2.8, D = 3.5
   b A = 1, B = 2, C = 3, D = 4
3 a 12   b 8   c 5

4.2 Conversions of length, mass and capacity

Multiplying and dividing by 10, 100 and 1000

1 a 50   b 430   c 7600
2 a 9   b 30   c 6
3 a 4.60   b 460   c 734   d 7340
4 a 5.1   b 0.51   c 8.71   d 0.871

Converting measures of length

1 10 mm
2 a cm   b km   c m   d mm
3 a $2 cm = 2 × 10 = 20 mm$ b $6.5 cm = 65 mm$
   c $40 mm = 40 ÷ 10 = 4 cm$ d $48 mm = 4.8 cm$
4 a $5 m = 5 × 100 = 500 cm$
   b $3 m = 300 cm$
   c $314 cm = 314 ÷ 100 = 3.14 m$
   d $482 cm = 4.82 m$
   e $7 km = 7 × 1000 = 7000 m$
   f $2 km = 2000 m$
   g $9200 m = 9200 ÷ 1000 = 9.2 km$
   h $2300 m = 2.3 km$
5 Anita
6 a 345 cm, 3.5 m, 400 cm, 4.2 m
   b 2.12 m, 234 cm, 3 m, 303 cm

Converting measures of mass and capacity

1 a $2.3 kg = 2.3 × 1000 = 2300 g$
   b $4.6 kg = 4600 g$
   c $1200 g = 1200 ÷ 1000 = 1.2 kg$
   d $6400 g = 6.4 kg$

2 a ml   b litres   c litres
3 a $9.4 litres = 9.4 × 1000 = 9400 ml$
   b $7.5 litres = 7500 ml$
   c $7320 ml = 7320 ÷ 1000 = 7.32 litres$
   d $2410 ml = 2.41 litres$
4 a cm   b g   c ml

4.3 Scales and measures

Scale drawing

1 a A = 1.2 cm, B = 2.5 cm, C = 6.2 cm
   b A = 12 mm, B = 25 mm, C = 62 mm
   c i 6.2 cm   ii 62 mm
2 a 4 cm   b 4 m
3 a 2 cm   b 2 m
4 Accurately drawn lines of lengths:
   a 3 cm   b 5 cm   c 4.5 cm

Reading simple scales counting by 1 or 0.1

1 a 300 ml   b 2 °C   c 300 g
2 a 5 °C   b 12 ml   c 13 cm
3 a 1.3 litres   b 0.8 kg

More scales

1 a 60   b 300
2 a 2, 4, **6**, **8**, 10, **12**
   b 10, **20**, **30**, 40, **50**, 60
   c 25, 50, **75**, 100, **125**, **150**
   d 200, **250**, 300, **350**
   e 1, **1.5**, 2, **2.5**, 3, **3.5**
   f 100, **125**, 150, **175**, 200
   g 100, **150**, 200, **225**, **275**, 300
   h 150, **153**, **155**, **158**, 160
3 a 0.3 m, 0.7 m   b 30 cm, 70 cm
   c 0.1 kg, 0.8 kg   d 100 g, 800 g
   e 0.2 litres, 0.9 litres   f 200 ml, 800 ml
4 a 250 g, 500 g, 750 g   b 250 ml, 500 ml, 750 ml
   c 400 g, 600 g, 800 g   d 200 ml, 600 ml, 800 ml
5 a 320
   b i 550   ii 525   iii 575

4.4 Working with decimals mentally

Multiplying decimals

1 a $0.1 = 1 ÷ 10$ b $0.2 = 2 ÷ 10$
   c $0.3 = 3 ÷ 10$ d $0.4 = 4 ÷ 10$
   e $0.01 = 1 ÷ 100$ f $0.02 = 2 ÷ 100$
   g $0.03 = 3 ÷ 100$ h $0.04 = 4 ÷ 100$
2 a 1.2   b 3.5   c 7.2   d 2.7
   e 0.12   f 0.35   g 0.72   h 0.27
3 a 12   b 1.2   c 0.12   d 12
   e 1.2   f 0.12   g 1.2   h 0.12
   i 12   j 1.2   k 0.12   l 12
   m 0.12   n 1.2   o 12   p 0.12
   q 1.2   r 12

Using partitioning to multiply

1 $5 × 30 = 5 × 3 × 10$
   $7 × 800 = 7 × 8 × 100$
   $7 × 90 = 7 × 9 × 10$
   $4 × 50 = 4 × 5 × 10$
   $8 × 300 = 8 × 3 × 100$
2 a 150   b 5600   c 630
   d 200   e 2400
3 a 68   b 63   c 85
4 a 265   b 26.5   c 213   d 21.3
   e 196   f 19.6   g 368   h 36.8

Using one calculation to work out another

1 a 153
   b i 15.3   ii 15.3   iii 1.53   iv 1.53
2 a 22.4   b 2.24
   c $32 × 0.7 = 32 × 7 ÷ 10 = 224 ÷ 10 = 22.4$

4.5 Working with decimals

Adding and subtracting decimals

1 a 0.5   b 2.3   c 1.1   d 4.9
   e 0.8   f 4.5   g 0.8   h 5.0

2   **a** 7.3   **b** 4.4   **c** 10.5   **d** 9.0
    e 1.3   **f** 3.9

Decimal column addition and subtraction

1   **a** 34.8   **b** 89.2   **c** 147.8   **d** 113.3
2   **a** 1.8   **b** 12.6   **c** 36.2   **d** 12.4

Multiplying decimals

1   **a** 12.6   **b** 21.7   **c** 40.8   **d** 24.8

Dividing decimals

1   **a** 0.8   **b** 0.5   **c** 0.9   **d** 0.7
2   **a** 17.1   **b** 7.1   **c** 7.2   **d** 3.3
3   **a** £6.50 **b** £1.60 **c** £4.15 **d** £0.11
4   36

4.6 Perimeter

Perimeter of squares and rectangles

1   **a** A 16 cm, B 16 cm
    b A 5 cm, 3 cm, 5 cm, 3 cm; B 2 cm, 6 cm, 2 cm, 6 cm.
       Opposite sides are equal lengths
    c A 16 cm, B 16 cm, yes
2   **a** all 8 cm   **b** 32 cm
3   **a** 3 cm, 5 cm **b** 16 cm
4   **a** 14 cm   **b** 12 cm   **c** 14 cm   **d** 14 cm
5   16 cm
6   128 cm
7   18.8 m
8   159.4 cm

Perimeter of shapes made from rectangles

1   **a** $A = 9$ cm, $B = 7$ cm   **b** 32 cm
2   **a** $A = 2.5$ m, $B = 1.8$ m, $C = 5$ m
    b 21.4 m

Perimeter of polygons

1   **a** pentagon: all sides 2 cm, hexagon all sides 2 cm
    b pentagon 10 cm; hexagon 12 cm
2   **a** 36 cm   **b** 25 cm   **c** 24 cm   **d** 36 cm

4.7 Area

Finding area by counting squares

1   **a** A: 4 cm², B: 8 cm²
    b A: 4 cm², B: 8 cm², yes, it is the same
2   A: 1 cm²   B: 4 cm²   C: 6 cm²   D: 6 cm²
    E: 12 cm²   F: 0.5 cm²   G: 2 cm²

Area of rectangles and squares

1   **a** Area = 12 cm × 4 cm = 48 cm²
    b Area = 6 cm × 3 cm = 18 cm²
    c Area = 5 cm × 5 cm = 25 cm²
2   **a** 16 cm²   **b** 16 cm²   **c** 14 cm²
    d 40 cm²
3   **a** 24.4 cm² **b** 27.5 cm² **c** 25.42 cm² **d** 2856 mm²
4   **a** A: 1 cm², B: 4 cm², C: 9 cm²
    b 16 cm²
    c Square numbers
5   **a** 81 cm²   **b** 625 mm² **c** 0.49 cm² **d** 5.76 mm²
6   a, b, c   Student's own drawings

Area of shapes made from rectangles

1   Area 1: length = 6 cm, width = 4 cm
    Area = 6 cm × 4 cm = 24 cm²
    Area 2: length = 5 cm, width = 2 cm
    Area = 5 cm × 2 cm = 10 cm²
    Total area = Area 1 + Area 2
        = 24 cm² + 10 cm²
        = 34 cm²
2   **a** 50 cm²   **b** 39 cm²   **c** 132 cm²

4.8 More units of measure

Choosing suitable units of measure

1   **a** m, km, mm **b** litres, ml   **c** g, kg
2   **a** mm, cm, m, km   **b** mm², cm², m², km²
3   **a** km²   **b** cm²   **c** m²
    d mm²   **e** cm² (or mm²)

Converting metric units

1   **a** 3 t = 3 × 1000 = 3000 kg
    b 4 t = 4 × 1000 = 4000 kg
    c 7000 kg = 7000 ÷ 1000 = 7 t
    d 5000 kg = 5000 ÷ 1000 = 5 t
    e 9 t = 9 × 1000 = 9000 kg
    f 12 000 kg = 12 000 ÷ 1000 = 12 t
2   **a** 5 ha = 5 × 10 000 = 50 000 m²
    b 80 000 m² = 80 000 ÷ 10 000 = 8 ha
    c 7 ha = 7 × 10 000 = 70 000 m²
    d 40 000 m² = 40 000 ÷ 10 000 = 4 ha
    e 15 ha = 15 × 10 000 = 150 000 m²
    f 220 000 m² = 220 000 ÷ 10 000 = 22 ha
3   **a** 4 ml = 4 cm³   **b** 6 cm³ = 6 ml
    c 12 ml = 12 cm³   **d** 22 cm³ = 22 ml
4   **a** 5 litres = 5 × 1000 = 5000 ml = 5000 cm³
    b 7 litres = 7 × 1000 = 7000 ml = 7000 cm³
    c 12 000 cm³ = 12 000 ml = 12 000 ÷ 1000 = 12 litres
    d 8000 cm³ = 8000 ml = 8000 ÷ 1000 = 8 litres
5   **a** 570 000 m² **b** 120 000 m² **c** 5

Converting metric and imperial measures

1   **a** 60 cm   **b** 1 ft   **c** 4 ft
    d 360 cm   **e** 240 cm   **f** 12 ft
2   **a** 11.2 km **b** 5 miles   **c** 22.4 km
    d 7.5 miles **e** 35.2 km   **f** 15 miles
3   150 cm
4   **a** 40 000 ml **b** 40 000 cm³
5   **a** 6000 kg   **b** 5400 kg
    c **i** 0.6 t   **ii** 600 kg

Unit 5 Fractions and percentages

5.1 Comparing fractions

Using fractions to describe parts of shapes

1   $\frac{1}{7}$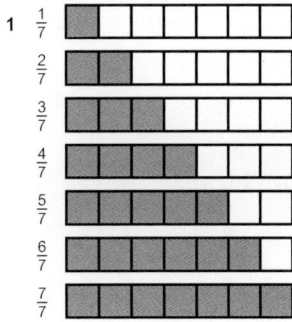

   $\frac{2}{7}$

   $\frac{3}{7}$

   $\frac{4}{7}$

   $\frac{5}{7}$

   $\frac{6}{7}$

   $\frac{7}{7}$

2   A and E; B and D, C and F

3   a $\frac{2}{6} = \frac{1}{3}$ b $\frac{5}{9}$ c $\frac{6}{12} = \frac{1}{2}$

   d $\frac{3}{8}$ e $\frac{3}{8}$

Ordering fractions

1   a   i $\frac{3}{5}$ ii $\frac{2}{5}$ iii $\frac{4}{5}$

   b $\frac{2}{5}, \frac{3}{5}, \frac{4}{5}$

2   Angie

3   a, b

   $\frac{1}{4}$

   $\frac{3}{4}$

   $\frac{2}{4}$

   c $\frac{1}{4}, \frac{2}{4}, \frac{3}{4}$

4   a $\frac{1}{8}, \frac{3}{8}, \frac{7}{8}$

   b $\frac{3}{10}, \frac{7}{10}, \frac{9}{10}$

   c $\frac{1}{12}, \frac{5}{12}, \frac{7}{12}, \frac{11}{12}$

   d $\frac{2}{13}, \frac{4}{13}, \frac{5}{13}, \frac{7}{13}, \frac{11}{13}$

5   a   i $\frac{3}{6} = \frac{1}{2}$ ii $\frac{3}{8}$ iii $\frac{3}{7}$ iv $\frac{3}{9} = \frac{1}{3}$

   b $\frac{3}{6}, \frac{3}{7}, \frac{3}{8}, \frac{3}{9}$

5.2 Simplifying fractions

Changing improper fractions to mixed numbers

1   a   2

   b   i   3   ii   4   ii   5

2   a $1\frac{1}{5}$ b $1\frac{2}{5}$ c $1\frac{3}{5}$

   d $1\frac{4}{5}$ e   2   f $2\frac{1}{5}$

3   a $1\frac{1}{7}$ b $1\frac{2}{7}$ c $1\frac{3}{7}$ d $1\frac{4}{7}$

   e $3\frac{1}{3}$ f $3\frac{2}{3}$ g   4   h $4\frac{1}{3}$

Equivalent fractions

1   a $\frac{1}{2}$ b $\frac{2}{4}$ c $\frac{4}{8}$ d $\frac{6}{12}$

   e $\frac{8}{16}$

2   a   i $\frac{2}{3}$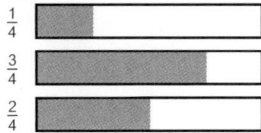

   ii $\frac{4}{5}$

   iii $\frac{3}{6}$

   iv $\frac{8}{10}$

   v $\frac{4}{8}$

   vi $\frac{6}{9}$

   b $\frac{2}{3} = \frac{6}{9}, \frac{4}{5} = \frac{8}{10}, \frac{3}{6} = \frac{4}{8}$

3   a $\frac{1}{2} = \frac{5}{10}$ b $\frac{1}{4} = \frac{2}{8}$

   c $\frac{2}{3} = \frac{4}{6}$ d $\frac{2}{5} = \frac{4}{10}$

4   a $\frac{2}{6} = \frac{1}{3}$ b $\frac{2}{8} = \frac{1}{4}$

   c $\frac{3}{9} = \frac{1}{3}$ d $\frac{6}{9} = \frac{2}{3}$

5.3 Working with fractions

Adding fractions

1   a $\frac{2}{3}$ b $\frac{2}{7}$ c $\frac{2}{9}$ d $\frac{2}{11}$

2   a $\frac{2}{4} = \frac{1}{2}$ b $\frac{2}{6} = \frac{1}{3}$ c $\frac{2}{8} = \frac{1}{4}$

3   a $\frac{3}{5}$ b $\frac{5}{7}$ c $\frac{7}{9}$

4   a $\frac{4}{8} = \frac{1}{2}$ b $\frac{3}{6} = \frac{1}{2}$ c $\frac{5}{10} = \frac{1}{2}$

   d $\frac{3}{9} = \frac{1}{3}$ e $\frac{8}{12} = \frac{2}{3}$ f $\frac{5}{15} = \frac{1}{3}$

Subtracting fractions

1   a $\frac{4}{5} - \frac{1}{5} = \frac{3}{5}$ b $\frac{4}{5} - \frac{2}{5} = \frac{2}{5}$ c $\frac{4}{5} - \frac{3}{5} = \frac{1}{5}$

   d $\frac{5}{6} - \frac{1}{6} = \frac{4}{6}$ e $\frac{5}{6} - \frac{2}{6} = \frac{3}{6}$ f $\frac{5}{6} - \frac{3}{6} = \frac{2}{6}$

   g $\frac{5}{6} - \frac{4}{6} = \frac{1}{6}$

2   a $\frac{4}{5}$ b $\frac{3}{5}$ c $\frac{2}{5}$ d $\frac{1}{5}$

   e $\frac{5}{6}$ f $\frac{6}{7}$ g $\frac{7}{8}$ h $\frac{8}{9}$

3   $\frac{1}{6}$

Finding a fraction of a quantity

1   a   To find $\frac{1}{3}$ divide by 3

    i $\frac{1}{3}$ of $30 = 30 \div 3 = 10$ ii $\frac{1}{3}$ of $60 = 60 \div 3 = 20$

   b   To find $\frac{1}{4}$ divide by 4

    i $\frac{1}{4}$ of $20 = 20 \div 4 = 5$ ii $\frac{1}{4}$ of $40 = 40 \div 4 = 10$

   c   To find $\frac{1}{5}$ divide by 5

    i $\frac{1}{5}$ of $20 = 20 \div 5 = 4$ ii $\frac{1}{5}$ of $40 = 40 \div 5 = 8$

2   a   10   b   4   c   12   d   6

   e   70   f   9   g   3   h   100

3   a   £5   b   £15

5.4 Fractions and decimals

Converting between fractions and decimals

1. a 0.3   b 0.03   c 0.5   d 0.05
   e 0.31   f 0.33   g 0.34   h 0.11
2. a 0.06   b 0.6   c 6   d 0.08
   e 0.8   f 8

3. a $0.4 = \frac{4}{10}$ $0.04 = \frac{4}{100}$ $0.44 = \frac{44}{100}$

   b $0.5 = \frac{5}{10}$ $0.05 = \frac{5}{100}$ $0.55 = \frac{55}{100}$

   c $0.6 = \frac{6}{10}$ $0.06 = \frac{6}{100}$ $0.66 = \frac{66}{100}$

   d $0.7 = \frac{7}{10}$ $0.07 = \frac{7}{100}$ $0.77 = \frac{77}{100}$

4. a $\frac{1}{100}$ b $\frac{1}{10}$ c $\frac{1}{50}$ d $\frac{1}{5}$

   e $\frac{2}{25}$ f $\frac{4}{5}$ g $\frac{3}{25}$ h $\frac{7}{20}$

Writing one number as a fraction of another

1. a i   b iii   c ii   d iv

2. a $\frac{3}{4}$

   b $\frac{2}{7}$

   c $\frac{2}{6}$

5.5 Understanding percentages

Understanding percentages

1. a 10%   b 40%   c 70%   d 62%
   e 11%   f 44%   g 1%   h 16%
   i 83%

Converting percentages to fractions and decimals

1. a $91\% = \frac{91}{100} = 0.91$ b $23\% = \frac{23}{100} = 0.23$

   c $37\% = \frac{37}{100} = 0.37$ d $33\% = \frac{33}{100} = 0.33$

   e $71\% = \frac{71}{100} = 0.71$ f $97\% = \frac{97}{100} = 0.97$

2. a 0.34   b 0.92   c 0.18
   d 0.45   e 0.95

3. a $50\% = \frac{50}{100} = \frac{1}{2}$ b $25\% = \frac{25}{100} = \frac{1}{4}$

   c $30\% = \frac{30}{100} = \frac{3}{10}$ d $45\% = \frac{45}{100} = \frac{9}{20}$

   e $40\% = \frac{40}{100} = \frac{2}{5}$ f $14\% = \frac{14}{100} = \frac{7}{50}$

Converting decimals to percentages

1. a $0.54 = \frac{54}{100} = 54\%$ b $0.28 = \frac{28}{100} = 28\%$

   c $0.07 = \frac{7}{100} = 7\%$

2. a $0.1 = \frac{1}{10} = \frac{10}{100} = 10\%$

   b $0.3 = \frac{3}{10} = \frac{30}{100} = 30\%$

   c $0.9 = \frac{9}{10} = \frac{90}{100} = 90\%$

5.6 Percentages of amounts

Calculating 50%, 25% and 75%

1. a $30 \div 2 = 15$ b $300 \div 2 = 150$
   c $12 \div 2 = 6$ d $120 \div 2 = 60$
2. a £5   b 15p   c 4 miles   d 6 cm
3. a £30   b 24 kg   c 12 miles
   d 18 cm   e 1500 kg   f 60 litres

Calculating 10%, 20%, 30%, ...

1. a 3   b 30   c 12
   d 120   e 360   f 36
2. a 7 cm   b £40   c 19 g
   d 2 miles   e 5p   f 33 ml
3. a £4   b £6   c £8
   d £14   e £18
4. a 50   b 150   c 250   d 400
   e 500

Calculating 1%

1. a 1% of $200 = 200 \div 100 = 2$
   b $2000 \div 100 = 20$
   c 4   d 40   e 23   f 33
2. a 4 cm   b 12 g   d 19 mm
   e 30 miles   f 7p   g £200

Unit 6 Probability

6.1 The language of probability

Probability in words

1 A : 4   B : 2   C : 1
     D : 5   E : 3

2 impossible, unlikely, even chance, likely, certain

3 **a** likely   **b** unlikely   **c** even chance
     d certain   **e** impossible

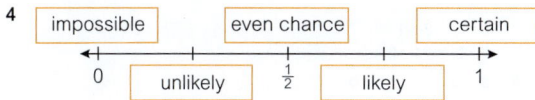

4

impossible		even chance			certain

0   unlikely $\frac{1}{2}$ likely   1

5 **a** circle with 3 segments shaded
     b circle with 1 or 2 segments shaded
     c circle with all segments shaded

Probability scale from 0 to 1

1 **a** 0.2   **b** 0.6   **c** 20%
     d 40%   **e** 90%   **f** $\frac{3}{10}$
     g $\frac{8}{10}$ **h** $\frac{1}{4}$ **i** $\frac{3}{4}$

2 impossible   even chance   certain
     c   a   b   d

0   0.5   1
0% $\frac{1}{2}$ 100%

3 **a** 0   **b** 1

6.2 Calculating probability

Probability where all the outcomes are different

1 **a** red, blue, yellow, white
     b 4   **c** 1   **d** $\frac{1}{4}$ (or 0.25, 25%)

2 **a** 1, 2, 3, 4, 5, 6   **b** $\frac{1}{6}$

3 **a** M, A, T, H, S   **b** $\frac{1}{5}$

4 $\frac{1}{2}$ (or 0.5, 50%)

Probability where some outcomes are the same

1 white, white, white, white, white, black, black, black

2 H, E, L, L, O

3 1, 1, 2, 3

4 **a** red, blue, blue
     b $\frac{2}{3}$

5 **a** A, A, O, R, A
     b $\frac{3}{5}$ (or 0.6, 60%)

6 **a** $\frac{1}{5}$ **b** $\frac{2}{5}$

7 $\frac{2}{6}$

6.3 More probability calculations

Probability notation

1 **a** $\frac{1}{3}$ **b** $\frac{1}{3}$ **c** $\frac{1}{3}$

2 **a** $\frac{1}{5}$ **b** $\frac{1}{5}$ **c** $\frac{1}{5}$

3 **a** $\frac{1}{6}$ **b** $\frac{1}{6}$ **c** $\frac{1}{6}$

Probability of A or B

1 **a** $\frac{1}{7}$ **b** $\frac{2}{7}$ **c** $\frac{3}{7}$

2 **a** $\frac{1}{6}$ **b** $\frac{1}{6}$ **c** $\frac{2}{6}$

3 **a** $\frac{1}{3}$ **b** $\frac{2}{3}$ **c** 1

Probability of an event not happening

1 **a** $\frac{6}{8}$ (or $\frac{3}{4}$)
     b Yes. P(not blue) is the probability of everything not blue.

2 **a** 25%   **b** 100%   **c** 75%

3 **a** **i** $\frac{3}{5}$ **ii** $\frac{2}{5}$ **iii** $\frac{2}{5}$
     b P(not 2) = P(3 or 4)

6.4 Experimental probability

Experimental probability as a fraction

1 $\frac{4}{16} = \frac{1}{4}$

2 **a** 7   **b** 20   **c** $\frac{7}{20}$

3 **a** 7   **b** $\frac{2}{7}$ **c** $\frac{4}{7}$ **d** $\frac{1}{7}$

4 **a** $\frac{19}{20}$ **b** $\frac{1}{20}$

Experimental probability as a percentage

1 **a** $\frac{17}{100} = 17\%$ **b** $\frac{12}{50} = \frac{24}{100} = 24\%$
     c $\frac{7}{25} = \frac{28}{100} = 28\%$ **d** $\frac{11}{20} = \frac{55}{100} = 55\%$
     e $\frac{3}{10} = \frac{30}{100} = 30\%$ **f** $\frac{11}{50} = \frac{22}{100} = 22\%$

2 **a** $\frac{3}{10}$ **b** $\frac{2}{10}$ **c** $\frac{5}{10}$
     d 30%   **e** 20%   **f** 50%

3 **a** 100
     b $\frac{34}{100} = 34\%$ **c** $\frac{6}{100} = 6\%$ **d** $\frac{60}{100} = 60\%$

4 **a** $\frac{11}{20} = \frac{55}{100} = 55\%$ **b** $\frac{9}{20} = \frac{45}{100} = 45\%$

6.5 Expected outcomes

Calculating probability

1 **a** There are different numbers of red and white balls, so the probability of picking one colour is different from the probability of picking the other colour.
     b **i** $\frac{1}{4}$ (= 25%)   **ii** $\frac{3}{4}$ (= 75%)

2 **a** $\frac{1}{6}$ **b** $\frac{1}{2}$ **c** $\frac{1}{2}$
     d $\frac{1}{2}$ (2, 3, 5)   **e** $\frac{1}{3}$ (1, 4)

3 $\frac{1}{6}$

Expected outcomes

1 **a** $\frac{1}{2}$ of 120 = 120 ÷ 2 = 60
     b $\frac{1}{3}$ of 120 = 120 ÷ 3 = 40
     c $\frac{1}{4}$ × 120 = 120 ÷ 4 = 30
     d $\frac{1}{5}$ × 120 = 120 ÷ 5 = 24
     e $\frac{1}{6}$ × 120 = 120 ÷ 6 = 20
     f $\frac{1}{10}$ × 120 = 120 ÷ 10 = 12

2 **a** 30   **b** 60   **c** 50   **d** 67.5
3 **a** 1   **b** 2   **c** 10   **d** 100
4 **a** 1   **b** 3   **c** 4   **d** 10
5 **a** 80   **b** 20   **c** 4

Calculating probability and expected outcomes

1 **a** 79
     b **i** 0.79   **ii** 0.21

2 **a** 20   **b** $\frac{20}{200} = \frac{1}{10}$

Unit 7 Ratio and proportion

7.1 Direct proportion

Working with one item

1 a i 3 kg × 2   ii 3 kg × 6
   b i 6 kg   ii 18 kg
2 a 100p (= £1.00)
   b 150p (= £1.50)
3 a £70   b £350   c £1400
4 a 30 g ÷ 2
   b 15 g
5 a divide by 2
   b 200 g
6 8p

Working out information about multiple items

1 a For 1 person you need 100 ÷ 2 = 50 g of flour.
   b For 5 people you need 50 × 5 = 250 g of flour.
2 a £50   b £100
3 a £7   b £35
4 a ¥8   b ¥480
5 a 30 g flour, 10 g butter, 20 g sugar
   b 300 g flour, 100 g butter, 200 g sugar
6 £4

7.2 Writing ratios

Ratios in tile and bead patterns

1 a ■ □ □

   b i 1   ii 2
   c For every 1 black tile there are 2 white tiles.
2 a 1 : 3   b 1 : 5   c 2 : 1   d 3 : 2
3 a 2 : 3   b 4 : 2   c 4 : 3   d 1 : 5
4 a Students' own answers, could include:

   etc.
   b Add the two parts of the ratio 1 + 4 = 5
5 3 : 5

Simplifying ratios

1 a 1 : 3   b 5 : 7   c 2 : 5
   d 1 : 3   e 2 : 3   f 2 : 3
2 a purple : white = 3 : 6 = 1 : 2
   b purple : white = 2 : 2 = 1 : 1
   c purple : white = 2 : 4 = 1 : 2

3

Ratio	Highest common factor	Simplified ratio
2 : 4	2	1 : 2
4 : 6	2	2 : 3
6 : 8	2	3 : 4
8 : 10	2	4 : 5
3 : 6	3	1 : 2
6 : 9	3	2 : 3
9 : 12	3	3 : 4
4 : 8	4	1 : 2
8 : 12	4	2 : 3
12 : 16	4	3 : 4

7.3 Using ratios

Equivalent ratios

1 a 10 : 2   b 18 : 15   c 30 : 20
2 a i 2 : 6   ii 3 : 9   iii 4 : 12
   b 5 : 15, 6 : 18, 10 : 30, etc.
   c Yes. 11 ÷ 11 = 1, 33 ÷ 11 = 3
3 8 : 12 = 2 : 3
   15 : 20 = 3 : 4
   7 : 14 = 1 : 2
   9 : 3 = 3 : 1
   7 : 2 = 21 : 6
4 a 2   b 2   c 10
5 a 2 : 10   b 2 : 12   c 2 : 14   d 3 : 15
   e 3 : 18   f 3 : 21   g 4 : 6   h 6 : 9
   i 8 : 12

Using equivalent ratios to solve problems

1 a

Number of black beads	Number of red beads
1	2
2	4
3	6
4	8

   b i 1 : 2 = 8 : 16. Alex will need 16 red beads.
      ii 8 + 16 = 24 beads in total
2 a 12 children   b 18 children
   c 42 children
   d i 7 adults   ii 42 children
3 a 6 blue counters
   b 9 blue counters
   c 12 blue counters
4 a i 4 red counters
      ii 6 blue counters
   b i 8 red counters
      ii 12 blue counters
   c i 10 red counters
      ii 15 blue counters
5 9 green mugs

7.4 Ratios, proportions and fractions

Proportions as fractions

1 a $\dfrac{\text{number of yellow parts}}{\text{total number of parts}} = \dfrac{1}{5}$

   b $\dfrac{3}{5}$ c $\dfrac{1}{7}$ d $\dfrac{5}{8}$
2 a $\dfrac{1}{2}$ b $\dfrac{2}{3}$ c $\dfrac{3}{4}$ d $\dfrac{1}{2}$
3 a $\dfrac{3}{7}$ b $\dfrac{4}{7}$
4 a $\dfrac{2}{7}$ b $\dfrac{5}{7}$

Ratios and proportions as fractions

1 a 2 : 3
   b i The proportion of blue tiles $= \dfrac{2}{5}$

      ii The proportion of red tiles $= \dfrac{3}{5}$

2 a $3:4$ **b** $\frac{3}{7}$ **c** $\frac{4}{7}$

3 a

   b   **i** $\frac{1}{8}$ **ii** $\frac{7}{8}$

   c   He has used the number of black tiles, instead of the total number of tiles.

4 a $\frac{5}{8}$ **b** $\frac{3}{8}$

7.5 Proportions and percentages

Proportions as percentages

1 a $\frac{1}{10} = \frac{10}{100} = 10\%$

   b $\frac{2}{50} = \frac{4}{100} = 4\%$

   c $\frac{7}{10} = \frac{70}{100} = 70\%$

   d $\frac{6}{20} = \frac{30}{100} = 30\%$

   e $\frac{4}{25} = \frac{16}{100} = 16\%$

   f $\frac{3}{5} = \frac{60}{100} = 60\%$

2 a   41%   **b**   14%   **c**   30%
   d   45%   **e**   28%   **f**   40%

3   87%

4   42%

5 a $\frac{51}{100}$ **b**   51%

6 a $\frac{9}{10}$ **b**   90%

7 a   **i** $\frac{22}{50}$ **ii**   44%

   b   **i** $\frac{15}{25}$ **ii**   60%

   c   Tom

Ratios and proportions as percentages

1 a   blue : red = $3 : 7$
   b   **i**   proportion of blue tiles $= \frac{3}{10} = \frac{30}{100} = 30\%$

      ii   proportion of red tiles $= \frac{7}{10} = \frac{70}{100} = 70\%$

2 a $11 : 9$ **b**   55%   **c**   45%

3 a

   b   **i**   40%   **ii**   60%

Unit 8 Lines and angles

8.1 Measuring and drawing angles

Measuring angles

1 a 45°
   b 70°
2 a 45°
   b 50°
   c 20°
3 a 140°
   b 170°
4 a 120°
   b 100°
   c 150°
5 a 300°
   b 320°
   c 200°

Drawing angles

1 Angle drawn of 50°
2 Angle drawn of 65°

8.2 Lines, angles and triangles

Naming and describing lines, angles and triangles

1 a A:3 B:2 C:0
   b A:3 B:2 C:0
2 a Equilateral
   b Isosceles
   c Scalene
3 a Scalene
   b Isosceles
   c Equilateral
4 a QR = PQ
   b PR is not equal to PQ.
5 a BAC = ABC
   b ABC and BAC are not equal to ACB
6 a Parallel
   b Neither
   c Perpendicular
   d Parallel
   e Neither
   f Perpendicular
   g Neither
   h Parallel
7 a 1 pair of parallel lines
   b 2 pairs of parallel lines
   c No pairs of parallel lines
   d No pairs of parallel lines
   e 2 pairs of parallel lines
   f No pairs of parallel lines

Estimating angles

1 a C, D
   b A, E
   c A
2 a D
   b A, B, C
3 a 60°
   b 20°
   c 80°

8.3 Drawing triangles accurately

Drawing triangles accurately, with two sides and one angle given

1 Draw and label a correct triangle.
2 Draw lines of correct length.
3 Draw angles of correct size.
4 Draw and label a correct triangle.
5 Draw and label correct triangles.

Drawing triangles accurately, with two angles and one side given

1 Draw and label correct triangle.
2 Draw and label correct triangles.

8.4 Calculating angles

Angles on a straight line

1 a 120
   b 80
   c 60
   d 90
   e 100
   f 135
2 a 70°/110°
   b 50°/130°
   c 100°/80°
   d 130°/50°
3 Both angles always add up to 180°.
4 a 140°
   b 70°
   c 80°
   d 60°
   e 90°
   f 120°

Angles around a point

1 a 300
   b 260
   c 240
   d 270
   e 180
   f 120
2 a 60°
   b 240°
   c 130°
   d 320°

Vertically opposite angles

1 a 120°
   b 70°
   c 145°
   d 42°
2 a 100°
   b 100°
   c 80°
   d 80°
   e 90°
   f 90°
3 a $a = b = 50°$
   b $p = 40, q = 50°$

8.5 Angles in a triangle

Missing interior angles in a triangle

1 a 180°
   b 180°
   c 180°
   d They all add up to 180°.
2 a 70°
   b 135°
   c 40°
3 a 80°
   b 60°
   c 85°

Missing exterior angles in a triangle

1 a 180°, 180°,180°
   b All angles add up to 180°.
2 a 110°
   b 120°
   c 150°

8.6 Quadrilaterals

Properties of quadrilaterals

1 A, B, C, E, F
2 a A, D, E, F, G
   b A, D, F, G
   c A, C, F, G
   d A, C, E, F, G
   e B, C
   f B, C
   g C

Calculating missing angles in a quadrilateral

1 a 360°
   b 360°
   c 360°
   d 360°
2 Angles in a quadrilateral add up to 360°.
3 The angles add to 400° not 360°.
4 $a = 54°$
5 a 68°
   b 111°

Unit 9 Sequences and graphs

9.1 Sequences

Number sequence terms and rules

1   a   6   b   10   c   14   d   18
2   a   i   1   ii   21
    b   i   3   ii   11
    c   i   65   ii   55
    d   i   24   ii   16
3   a   +2   b   +3   c   +5
4   a   −2   b   −5   c   −3
5   a   5, 9   b   5, 7   c   5, 8   d   10, 7
6   a   Decreasing   b   Increasing
    c   Increasing   d   Decreasing

Number sequence problems

1   a   £12   b   £14   c   £16
    d   12, 14, 16, 18, 20, 22, 24
    e   7 weeks
2   a   £40   b   £35   c   Day 9

9.2 Pattern sequences

Pattern sequences and rules

1   a   +2 triangles   b   +1 square
    c   +2 dots   d   +3 dots
2   a

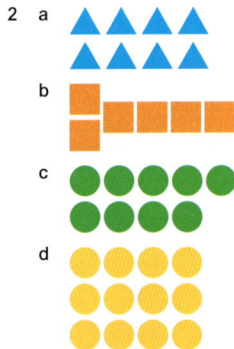

3   a

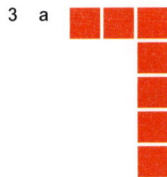

    b

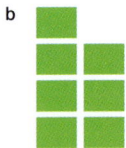

    c

Using tables for pattern sequences

1   a   i   5   ii   6   b   +1 counter
    c

Pattern number	1	2	3	4	5
Number of counters	4	5	6	7	8

2   a   i   5   ii   7   iii   9
    b   +2 squares
    c

Pattern number	1	2	3	4	5
Number of squares	5	7	9	11	13

3   a   +2 sticks
    b

Pattern number	1	2	3	4	5
Number of sticks	3	5	7	9	11

9.3 Coordinates and midpoints

Reading and plotting coordinates

1   a   1   b   5   c   10   d   5
    e   15   f   5   g   12   h   18
2   A (2, 4)   B (5, 1)   C (3, 3)   D (0, 5)   E (4, 0)
3

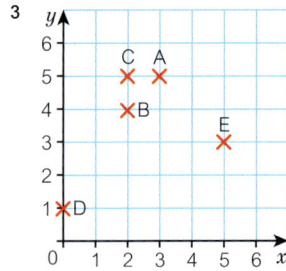

4   The points A and E are not in the same place because their x-coordinates are different and their y-coordinates are different.
5   a   −2   b   −7   c   −3   d   −8
6   A(−4, 3)   B(4, −2)   C(2, −3)   D(−2, −3)
    E(−1, −4)   F(0, −3)
7

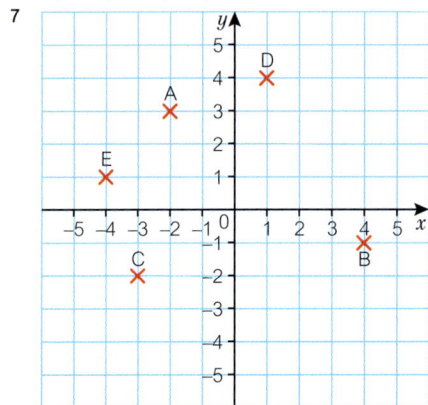

8   The points B and E are not in the same place because their x-coordinates are different and their y-coordinates are different.
9   a   (0, 0) (1, 2) (2, 4) (3, 6)
    b $y = 2x$
    c

x	0	1	2	3	4	5
y	0	2	4	6	8	10

Midpoints of a line segment

1   a, b, e

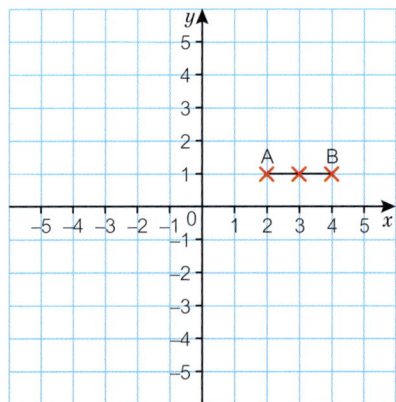

    c   2   d   1   e   (3, 1)

2 a, b, e

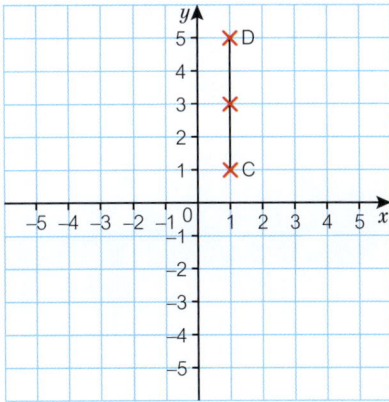

c 4   d 2   e (1, 3)

9.4 Extending sequences

Arithmetic sequences

1 a Yes   b Yes   c No   d No
2 a 9   b 20   c 4   d 2
3 a 5, +4   b 2, +5   c 35, −10   d 20, −3

Geometric sequences

1 a Yes   b Yes   c Yes   d Yes
       e No   f Yes
2 a 8, 16   b 6, 18   c 20, 10   d 10, 2

Sequences with two-step rules

1 a 3, 4, 6   b 2, 9, 30   c 7, 10, 16   d 4, 10, 22

9.5 Straight-line graphs

Graphs parallel to the axes and $y = x$

1 a, b, e

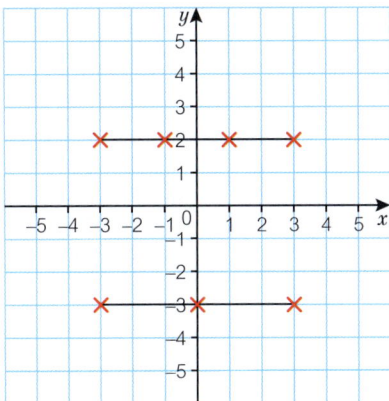

c $y = 2$
d Any one of (−2, 2), (0, 2), (2, 2)
e $y = −3$, any one of (−2, 3), (−1, 3), (1, 3), (2, 3)

2 a, b, e

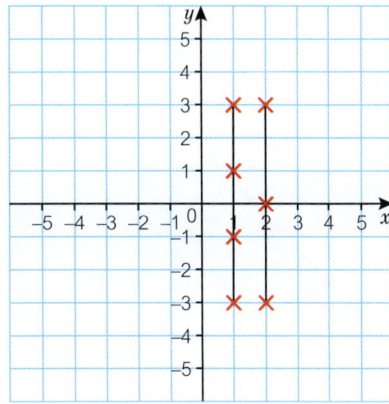

c $x = 1$
d Any one of (1, 2), (1, 0), (1, −2)
e $x = 2$, any one of (2, 2), (2, 1), (2, −1), (2, −2)

3 a, b

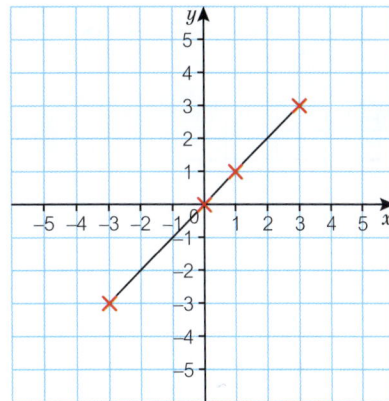

c $y = x$
d Any one of (−2, −2), (−1, −1), (2, 2)

Drawing a table of values and plotting straight line graphs

1 **a** 0   **b** 1   **c** 2

2 **a** 7, 8

b

x	0	1	2	3
y	5	6	7	8

c (0, 5), (1, 6), (2, 7), (3, 8)

d, e

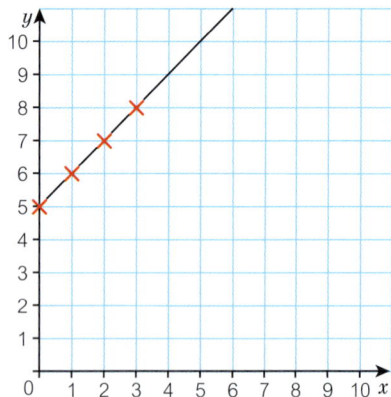

3 **a** 4, 6

b

x	0	1	2	3
y	0	2	4	6

c (0, 0), (1, 2), (2, 4), (3, 6)

d

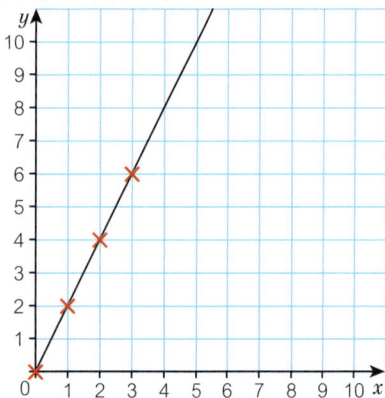

Finding the nth term

1 **a** +7   **b** +4   **c** ×3   **d** ×8

2 **a** $n + 7$ **b** $n + 4$ **c** $3n$ **d** $8n$

9.6 Position-to-term rules

Finding terms of a sequence using the position-to-term rule

1 **a** 8   **b** 6   **c** 4   **d** 10

2 **a** +1   **b** $n+3$

3 **a** 4, 5, 6, 7, 8

position (n)	1	2	3	4	5
term (n + 3)	4	5	6	7	8

b 10, 11, 12, 13, 14

position (n)	1	2	3	4	5
term (n + 9)	10	11	12	13	14

c 4, 8, 12, 16, 20

position (n)	1	2	3	4	5
term ($4n$)	4	8	12	16	20

d 10, 20, 30, 40, 50

position (n)	1	2	3	4	5
term ($10n$)	10	20	30	40	50

e 0, 1, 2, 3, 4

position (n)	1	2	3	4	5
term (n - 1)	0	1	2	3	4

Unit 10 Transformations

10.1 Congruency and enlargements

Congruence

1 a   iv   b   ii   c   i   d   iii

2 a   No, they are the same size but different shapes.

   b   Yes, they are the same shape and size.

   c   No, they are the same shape but different sizes.

3 a   3 cm   b   3 cm

Enlargement

1

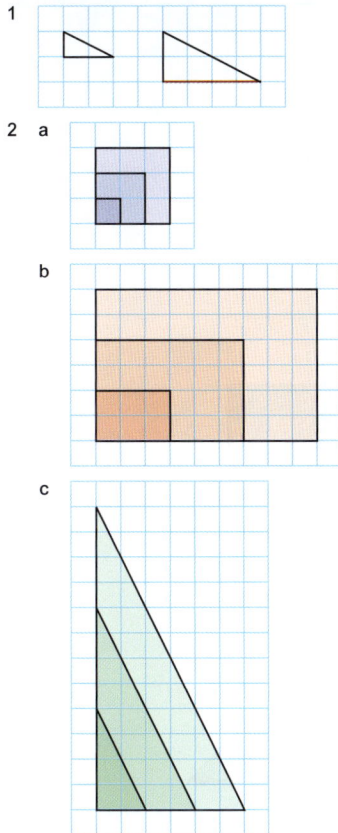

2 a

   b

   c

3 a   image height = scale factor × original height

       6 = 3 × 2

       image base = scale factor × original base

       3 = 3 × 1

       Scale factor = 3

   b   Scale factor = 2

10.2 Symmetry

Line symmetry

1 a   Yes   b   No   c   No

2 a   Yes   b   No   c   No   d   Yes

3 a   b

   c   d

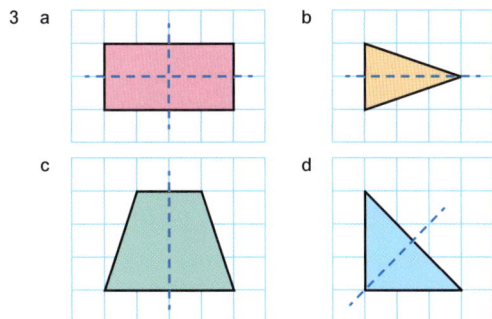

4 a   2   b   1   c   3   d   4

Rotational symmetry

1 a   2   b   2   c   1   d   4

2 a   4   b   2   c   1   d   3

Symmetry in 3D shapes

1   a, b

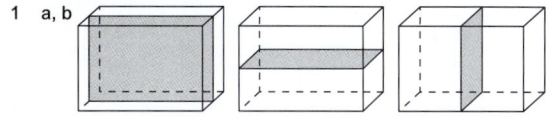

2   a, c and d

10.3 Reflection

Reflections in horizontal and vertical mirror lines

1   A

2   C

3

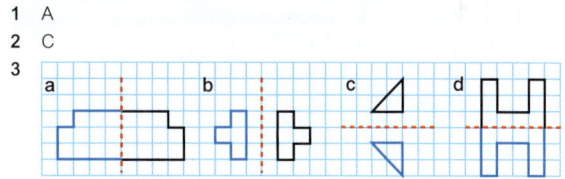

Reflections on a coordinate grid

1 a

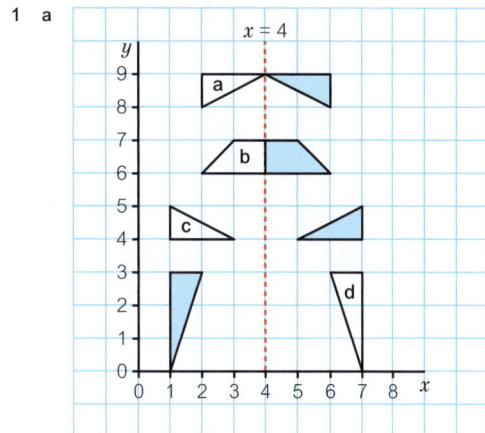

   b

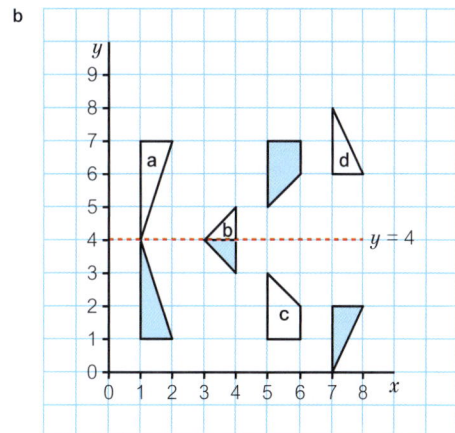

2

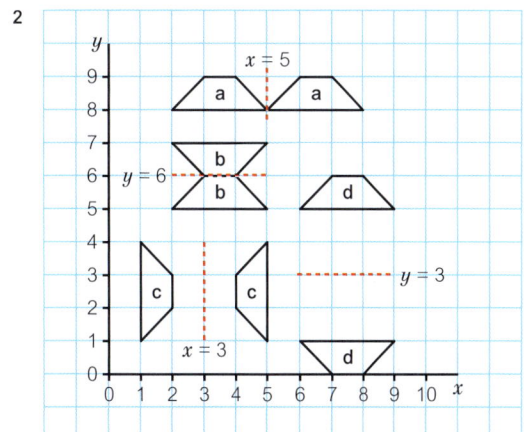

Reflections in diagonal lines

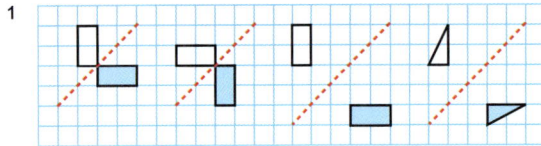

1

10.4 Rotation

Describing rotations

1 a ii   b i clockwise, iii anticlockwise
2 i a, e   ii b, f   ii c, d
3 a 90°   b anticlockwise
   c (3, 0)
   d 90° anticlockwise rotation about (3, 0)

Drawing rotations

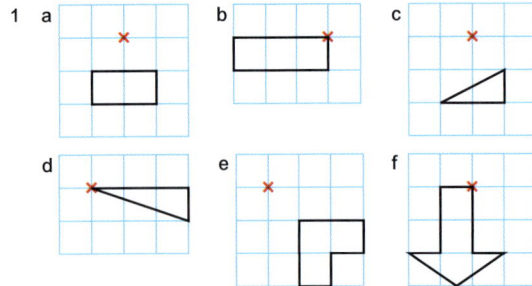

1

10.5 Translations and combined transformations

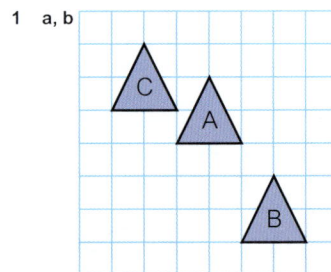

Describing translations

1 a A to B   2 squares up
   b A to C   3 squares right
   c B to C   3 squares right and 2 squares down
2 a A to B   4 squares left
   b A to C   4 squares down
   c A to D   3 squares right
   d A to E   5 squares up
   e B to A   4 squares right
   f C to A   4 squares up
   g D to A   3 squares left
   h E to A   5 squares down
3 a A to B   3 squares right and 1 square down
   b A to C   1 square right and 2 squares down
   c A to D   2 squares right and 2 squares up
   d A to E   3 squares left and 1 square down
   e B to C   2 squares left and 1 square down
   f B to D   1 square left and 3 squares up
   g B to E   6 squares left

Drawing translations

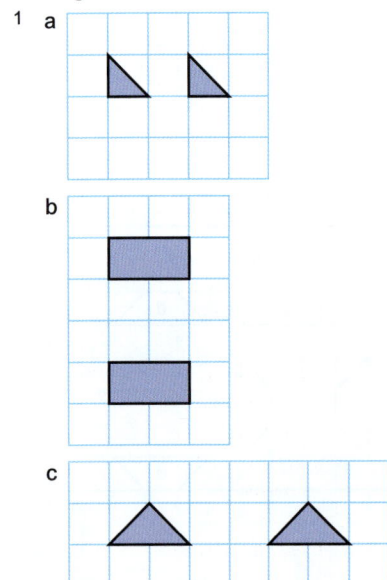

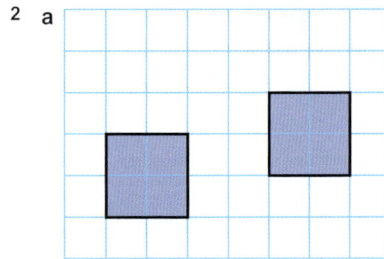

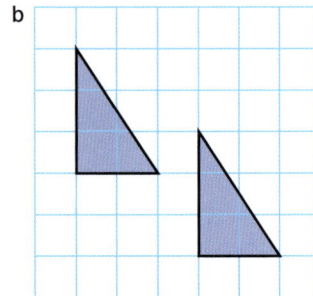

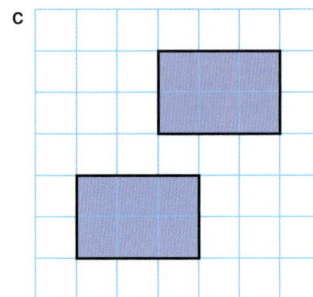

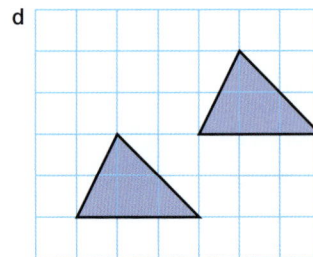

1 a

   b

   c

2 a

   b

   c

   d

Combined transformations

1 a, b

   c 2 squares left and 1 square up

159

Index